The Art of Reading as a Way of Life

The Art
of Reading
as a Way
of Life

On Nietzsche's Truth

Daniel T. O'Hara

Northwestern University Press
Evanston, Illinois

Northwestern University Press
www.nupress.northwestern.edu

Printed in the United States of America

10 9 8 7 6 5 4 3 2 1

Library of Congress Cataloging-in-Publication Data

O'Hara, Daniel T., 1948–
    The art of reading as a way of life : on Nietzsche's truth / Daniel T.
O'Hara.
        p. cm.
    Includes bibliographical references and index.
    ISBN 978-0-8101-2622-0 (trade cloth : alk. paper) 1. Nietzsche,
Friedrich Wilhelm, 1844–1900. 2. Truth. 3. Criticism. I. Title.
B3318.T78O33 2009
193—DC22

                                                            2009023498

CONTENTS

1. The Art of Reading as a Way of Life:
   An Introduction to Nietzsche's Truth   3

2. Experiments in Creative Reading:
   The Cambridge Nietzsche   17

3. Nietzsche's Passion in *The Gay Science:*
   An Experiment in Creative Reading   29

4. Nietzsche's Book for All and None:
   The Singularity of *Thus Spoke Zarathustra*   51

5. *Ecce Homo:* Nietzsche's Two Natures   73

6. Nietzsche's Critical Vortex: On the
   Global Tragedy of Theoretical Man   85

   Notes   107

   Index   117

The Art of Reading as a Way of Life

1

The Art of Reading as a Way of Life:
An Introduction to Nietzsche's Truth

I am a founding member of the editorial collective of *boundary 2: an international journal of literature and culture* and its longtime review editor, so what follows is not a cheap shot. But reading, as I write, the current issue's contents page is certainly instructive about the contemporary state of critical thinking. Here are the titles: "Timespace, Social Space, and the Question of Chinese Culture," "Foucault, Agamben: Theory and the Nazis," "*Andante ma non troppo e molto cantabile:* Audio (Il)literacy, or Beethoven's Triumphant Despair," "Grievable Life, Accountable Theory," "A Zombie Manifesto: The Nonhuman Condition in the Era of Advanced Capitalism," "The Pathology of Empire," "*Eis tin Polis:* Istanbul, December 1969," "Badiou's Truth and the Office of the Critic: Naming the Militant Multiples of the Void," "Immigrant Nation/Nativist State: Remembering Against the Archive of Forgetfulness," "Thomas Pynchon's *Against the Day.*" When the journal began in 1972, its focus was postmodern literature. Now, as can be seen, I am hardpressed to say what focus, if any, these titles demonstrate, aside from a general adversarial stance against whatever each essay takes as its object of criticism. I cannot claim that each essay constitutes its own alternative possible world and so is virtually incommensurate with every other, but certainly each essay appears idiosyncratic. I would claim that such idiosyncrasy is, paradoxically enough, representative. Given this prospect, just by the title alone, "A Zombie Manifesto: The Nonhuman Condition in the Era of Advanced Capitalism," may be the most representative in this paradoxical fashion. Since I am the author of "Badiou's Truth," I say this with a certain ambivalence, to say the least.

More important than this fragmentary and idiosyncratic nature of contemporary criticism is its growing failure to read texts closely. Instead of following out the logic of the text under consideration to the end, criticism exhibits snippets cut from many texts operating at many different levels. A snippet from a novel is spliced together with one from a film, an inter-text of a poem, one from a discourse, and/or a commonplace from the history of a genre. Similarly, the critical claims and their "hybridic" snippets often are loosely associated, and too often appear disconnected or connected only by self-consciously lame or strained assertions. So much is this the case that at times authors must confess to a purely parodic, indeed self-parodic, thrust of their efforts, as in the case of "A Zombie Manifesto":

> Borrowing the title and the spirit of [Donna] Haraway's "Cyborg Manifesto," one of the inaugurating texts of "posthuman theory," we argue here that the zombie can be made to speak only as a somewhat ironic discursive model. The zombie is anticatharsis; thus, "a zombie manifesto" is one that cannot call for positive change, it calls only for the destruction of the reigning model. Though our essay is at times tongue in cheek and aware of the absurdity of its own suggestions (rather like the zombie film genre itself, which often celebrates itself as "schlock" and "camp"), we are never mocking Haraway's pivotal and en-

4

during piece. We are greatly indebted to the "Cyborg Manifesto," and this is our homage. However, this essay is not a utopic fantasy in which man is liberated from the subject/object conundrum, nor is it a riotous celebration of the apocalypse that would ensue if humanity were able to get free of the subject/object bind. Mostly, it is an ironic imagining of what some of the philosophical concepts that have such currency in critical theory, such as "posthumanism," "negative dialectics," and the "rupture," which is awaited as the second coming of poststructuralism, might look like if incarnated in material form.[1]

Since I am also the author of two books entitled, respectively, *Radical Parody* and *Empire Burlesque,* and similarly oppose posthuman theory, I am sympathetic with the attempt here and do realize that the present scene of criticism is not good for encouraging the kind of reading I find missing generally from it. Nonetheless, what I find most disturbing is that the clearly noted performance dimension of criticism, as above, yields no real harvest of *new* knowledge. That is, critical technique is being employed, not for discovery and self-discovery, as a method of vision, but purely rhetorically, for persuasion purposes, in a professional debate.

We all know why this is the case now. The academic profession of criticism now runs entirely according to the rules of the late capitalistic game of the bottom line, so that all decisions about hiring, retention, tenure, promotion, merit, visibility, and so on are determined by the operation of this measure of value. The art of criticism, of reading and self-reading, what I am calling "the art of reading as a way of life," can hardly flourish in such conditions. Nevertheless, I am offering in this book just such a case of reading and self-reading in Nietzsche's case. Whether it is also my own case, only my readers can say. What now follows is specifically what Nietzsche shows us is involved in this art of reading as a way of life, but first I must preface my presentation by noting generally two more contemporary sources of inspiration for it: Paul de Man's work on Nietzsche in *Allegories of Reading: Figural Language in Rousseau, Nietzsche, Rilke, and Proust* (1979) and Alexander Nehamas's *Nietzsche: Life as Literature* (1985). My second authored book, *The Romance of Interpretation: Visionary Criticism from Pater to de Man* (1985), and my second edited collection, *Why Nietzsche Now?* (1985), detail both this inspiration and my differences from it.

Daybreak is the first text of Nietzsche's mature self-awareness. Its preface concludes famously with the following invocation of "slow reading":

> It is not for nothing that I have been a philologist, perhaps I am a philologist still, that is to say, a teacher of slow reading—in the end I also write slowly. Nowadays, it is not only my habit, it is also to my taste—a malicious taste, perhaps? —no longer to write anything which does not reduce to despair every sort of man who is "in a hurry." For philology is that venerable art which demands of its votaries one thing above all: to go aside, to take time, to become still, to become slow—it is a goldsmith's art and connoisseurship of the *word* which has nothing but delicate, cautious work to do and achieves nothing it does achieve except *lento*. But precisely for this reason it is more necessary than ever today, by precisely this means does it entice and enchant us most, in the midst of an age of "work," that is to say, of hurry, indecent and perspiring haste, which wants to "get everything done" at

> once, including every old or new book:—this art
> does not so easily get anything done, it teaches
> to read *well,* that is to say, to read slowly, deeply,
> looking cautiously before and aft, with reserva-
> tions, with doors left open, with delicate eyes
> and fingers . . . My patient friends, this book de-
> sires for itself only perfect readers and philolo-
> gists: *learn* to read me well![2]

In order to understand what Nietzsche means by philology here,
we have to understand, as James I. Porter has made clear in his
work, that it is as much a philology of the body as it is a critical reflection on physiology.[3] It was F. A. Lange's *History of Materialism*
in 1867 that first suggested to Nietzsche how this science could become a physiology of tropes.[4]

Throughout *Daybreak,* Nietzsche argues that the subject is a
variable mask of many conflicting drives. As such, we can use moral
imperatives to transform drives, or as we might say today after
Freud, sublimate them. In section 109, "Self-Mastery and Moderation and Their Ultimate Motive," Nietzsche enumerates and
briefly characterizes six defenses against the drives, including sublimation. What is important for me is his summary:

> Thus: avoiding opportunities, implanting regu-
> larity into the drive, engendering satiety and dis-
> gust with it and associating it with a painful idea
> (such as that of disgrace, evil consequences or
> offended pride), then dislocation of forces and
> finally a general weakening and exhaustion—
> these are the six methods [of defense]: *that* one
> *desires* to combat the vehemence of a drive at all,
> however, does not stand within our own power;
> nor does the choice of any particular method;

nor does the success or failure of this method.
What is clearly the case is that in this entire pro-
cedure our intellect is only the blind instrument
of *another drive* which is a *rival* of the drive whose
vehemence is tormenting us: whether it be the
drive to restfulness, or the fear of disgrace and
other evil consequences, or love. While "we" believe we are complaining about the vehemence
of a drive, at bottom it is one drive *which is complaining about another;* that is to say: for us to
become aware that we are suffering from the *vehemence* of a drive presupposes the existence of
another equally vehement or even more vehement drive and that a *struggle* is in prospect in
which our intellect is going to have to take sides.[5]

Here we see Nietzsche's basic theory of the subject in action as a
mask-play of drives and counter-drives, a differential agon or contest of drives for enhancement, discharge, or sole possession of the
psyche's power. We can only come to know each drive, which gives
us our momentary mood or state and conscious perspective, seri-
atim, in this antagonistic manner. While one vehement drive is
being treated in one of these six ways, the rival drive remains unknown to us until we fully play out the process of reading our experience. In this way, the quantity of affect carried by the drive can
ultimately discharge itself. Then the entire cycle repeats itself, in
principle, perpetually. In reading texts we are putting on display,
consciously or not, this ever-returning mask-play, and to read well,
for Nietzsche, means knowing this is so, because then we can shape
the play artfully.

This choice of the art of reading as a way of life is far from an
easy course to take:

Language and the prejudices upon which language is based are a manifold hindrance to us when we want to explain inner processes and drives; because of the fact, for example, that words really exist only for *superlative* degrees of these processes and drives, and where words are lacking, we are accustomed to abandon exact observation because exact thinking there becomes painful . . . *We are none of us* that which we appear to be in accordance with the states for which alone we have consciousness and words . . . and consequently we . . . *misunderstand* ourselves . . . we misread ourselves in this apparently most intelligible handwriting on the nature of our self. *Our opinion of ourselves, however,* which we have arrived at by this erroneous path, the so-called "ego," is thenceforth a fellow worker in the construction of our character and our destiny.[6]

Basically, Nietzsche is saying something here like, "We work in the dark, largely, and do what we can, if we are smart; the art of reading as a way of life is our passion, and our passion at times is too difficult to tell from madness."

The characteristic form that Nietzsche's art of reading takes is brilliantly exemplified in section 113 of *Daybreak,* which is on the striving for distinction:

The striving for distinction is the striving for domination over the next man, though it be a very indirect domination and only felt or even dreamed. There is a long scale of degrees of this

secretly desired domination, and a complete cat-
alogue of them would be almost the same thing
as a history of culture, from the earliest, still
grotesque barbarism up to the grotesqueries of
over-refinement and morbid idealism. The striving for distinction brings with it *for the next
man*—to name only a few steps on the ladder:
torment, then blows, then terror, then fearful as-
tonishment, then elevation, then joy, then cheer-
fulness, then laughter, then derision, then
mockery, then ridicule, then giving blows, then
imposing torment: here at the end of the ladder
stands the *ascetic* and *the martyr,* who feel the
highest enjoyment by himself enduring, as a
consequence of his drive for distinction, precisely that which, on the first step of the ladder,
his counterpart the *barbarian* imposes on others
on whom and before whom he wants to distin-
guish himself. The triumph of the ascetic over
himself, his glance turned inwards which beholds man split asunder into a sufferer and a
spectator, and henceforth gazes out into the
outer world in order to gather as it were wood
for his own pyre, this final tragedy of the drive
for distinction in which there is only one character burning and consuming himself—this is a
worthy conclusion and one appropriate to the
commencement: in both cases an unspeakable
happiness at the *sight of torment*! Indeed, happiness, conceived of as the liveliest feeling of
power, has perhaps been nowhere greater on
earth than in the souls of superstitious ascetics.[7]

Nietzsche, clearly using here the lens of the master-slave dialectic from Hegel's *Phenomenology of Spirit,* stresses the process of incorporation in the course of history that splits the subject into two, a double consciousness of sufferer and spectator. Whereas for Hegel this internalized dialectical opposition is ultimately resolved in the figure of the Sage who possesses and is possessed by Absolute knowledge at the end of history—that is, the dialectic is in principle closeable but in practice remains open—for Nietzsche the dialectic suddenly spirals upward and hovers open over the field of experience via a fantastic vision of the superhuman:

> I believe that in this whole species of inner experience we are now incompetent novices groping after the solution of riddles [in comparison to the Brahmins]: they knew more about these infamous refinements of self-enjoyment 4,000 years ago. The creation of the world: perhaps it was then thought of by some Indian dreamer as an ascetic operation on the part of a god! Perhaps the god wanted to banish himself into active and moving nature as into an instrument of torture, in order thereby to feel his bliss and power doubled! And supposing it was a god of love: what enjoyment for such a god to create *suffering* men, to suffer divinely and superhumanly from the ceaseless torment of the sight of them, and thus to tyrannise over himself! And even supposing it was not only a god of love, but also a god of holiness and sinlessness: what deliriums of the divine ascetic can be imagined when he creates sin and sinners and eternal damnation and a vast abode of eternal affliction and eternal groaning and sighing!—It is

not altogether impossible that the souls of Dante,
Paul, Calvin and their like [*such as Sade? such as
Nietzsche himself?* my questions] may also once
have penetrated the gruesome secrets of such
voluptuousness of power—and in face of such
souls one can ask: is the circle of striving for distinction really at end with the ascetic? Could this
circle not be run through again from the beginning, holding fast to the basic disposition of the
ascetic and at the same time in order thereby to
hurt *oneself,* in order then to triumph over oneself
and one's pity and to revel in an extremity of
power! Excuse these extravagant reflections on all
that may have been possible on earth through the
psychical extravagance of the lust for power![8]

What are we to make of this tragicomic, sadomasochistic spectacle?
Nietzsche is playing out to its momentary exhaustion these con-
joined twin-drives by both demonstrating the plausibility of their
being at the basis of holiness and love and ironically deifying them
in this Byronically romantic vision of a God only the divine Marquis could enjoy. The final "excuse me" sentence winks slyly at the
complicit reader.

Nietzsche accepts provisionally, prospectively, the wisdom of
Vico, that human beings can only know what they make, but with
his own Faustian twist: "The dominant principle of our thinking
would be that we can understand only that which we can *do.*"[9] This
is what the art of reading as a way of life just might deliver.

Experience and Invention explores this prospect experimentally:

However far a man may go in self-knowledge,
nothing however can be more incomplete than
this image of the totality of *drives* which consti-

tute his being. He can scarcely name even the
cruder ones: their number and strength, their
ebb and flood, their play and counterplay
among one another, and above all the laws of
their *nutriment* [*die Nahrung,* also "nourishment"], remain wholly unknown to him. This
nutriment is therefore a work of chance: our
daily experiences throw some prey in the way of
now this, now that drive, and the drive seizes it
eagerly; but the coming and going of these
events as a whole stands in no rational relationship to the nutritional requirements of the totality of the drives: so that the outcome will always
be twofold—the starvation and stunting of some
and the over-feeding of others.[10]

This is why Nietzsche recommends practicing the art of reading as
a way of life, as one drive after another plays out its rivalry and betrays itself differentially no matter what mask(s) it wears: we can
then learn something about ourselves and perhaps the changing
shape of that totality of drives, so that we can learn to redress at the
very least such imbalance.

Every moment of our lives sees some of the
polyp-arms of our being grow and others of
them wither, all according to the nutriment
which the moment does or does not bear with
it. Our experiences are, as already said, all in this
sense means of nourishment, but the nourishment is scattered indiscriminately without dis-
tinguishing between the hungry and those
already possessing a superfluity. As a consequence of this chance nourishment of the parts,

the whole, fully grown polyp will be something
just as accidental as its growth has been.[11]

Without a divine providence or progressive teleology informing the
process, with nothing but the blind necessity of accident, we must
practice the art of reading as a way of life if we are going to attend
to the event of the self-betraying truth of the drives, and so know
who and what we are, and more importantly what we may need
most to do in the future:

> To express it more clearly, suppose a drive finds
> itself at the point at which it desires gratifica-
> tion—or exercise of its strength, or discharge of
> its strength, or the saturation of an emptiness—
> these are all metaphors—it then regards every
> event of the day with a view to seeing how it can
> employ it for the attainment of its goal; whether
> a man is moving, or resting or angry or reading
> or speaking or fighting or rejoicing, the drive
> will in its thirst as it were taste every condition
> into which the man may enter, and as a rule will
> discover nothing for itself there and will have to
> wait and go on thirsting: in a little while it will
> grow faint, and after a couple of days or months
> of non-gratification it will wither away like a
> plant without rain.[12]

Consequently, Nietzsche continues, our dreams must compensate
for our experiences by their invention of fantasy-fulfillments. The
greater the freedom of these inventions, the more impoverished our
experiences.

Meanwhile, our judgments and evaluations can only be "images and fantasies based on a physiological process unknown to us,

a kind of acquired language for designating certain nervous stimuli
. . . [and] all our so-called consciousness is more or less fantastic
commentary on an unknown, perhaps unknowable, but felt text."[13]
This is why, for Nietzsche, his philology of the drives, which is also
a physiology of tropes, is so necessary for the art of reading as a way
of life. Each moment of everyday life potentially provides the symbolic scene and characters for the drama of our passions, affects,
and drives as the event of our unconscious truth becomes or may
become legible to us: "What then are our experiences? Much *more*
that which we put into them than that which they already contain!
Or must we go so far as to say: in themselves they contain nothing?
To experience is to invent?"[14] And to invent is to experiment.

In the chapters that follow, I trace critically, as I have done so
here via *Daybreak,* the current reception and translation of Nietzsche's corpus and then some of Nietzsche's boldest textual experiments in the art of reading as a way of life, including those in *The
Birth of Tragedy, The Gay Science, Thus Spoke Zarathustra, The Anti-
Christ,* and *Ecce Homo.* The shape of this critical tracing begins,
however, in the middle of his career with *The Gay Science,* moves on
to *Zarathustra,* which Nietzsche believed was the central work of
his life, continues by revaluing *Ecce Homo,* his final autobiograph-
ical statement about his life and career, and then concludes with a
comparative analysis of two works from the beginning and end of
that career, respectively, *The Birth of Tragedy* and *The Anti-Christ.*

In sum, the "progress" of my book is more like that of the spiral levitation of romantic irony discussed earlier in this introduction
than it is like the linear movement of conventional argument. In
this, among other ways, I attempt experimentally to remain true to
Nietzsche's truth. My repeated discussion and elaboration in these
chapters of Badiou's theory of the truth-event and the procedures
we devise to express our fidelity to that event is another such example. Badiou—and other theorists I discuss in this book—provide
me with tools for constructing an allegory of tragically exuberant

reading appropriate for Nietzsche, I hope, as well as for myself. If the finer points of identity with and difference between theorists are not always addressed in the process, this is because my aim in this book is less rote discussion and more exemplary (self-)revision of an imaginative nature. Similarly, I choose to read these texts by Nietzsche and not others, such as *Beyond Good and Evil* or *On the Genealogy of Morals*, of which there are many fine recent studies cited in the notes, because this is hardly the case for *Daybreak* or *The Anti-Christ* and, more importantly, because all of this is part of my own experimentalism *àpres le maître*—as is the timing and quantity of my consultation of the original German texts, and the regular use of large block quotations from them and their various English translations. As to this practice, I intend to lead the less scholarly reader, whom I also hope to interest, more easily into Nietzsche immersion, even as I would have all readers discover how Nietzsche in generous amounts, and from not just the expected texts, can be seen as being the best reader of Nietzsche. Besides, these days there are very few critical readings of the kind I propose and attempt to perform. Suffice it to say, Nietzsche's truth is what the philology of drives and physiology of tropes, the physiological philology and philological physiology, can disclose via the art of reading as a way of life.

2

Experiments in Creative Reading: The Cambridge Nietzsche

The ten volumes in the series of the Cambridge Texts in the History of Philosophy devoted to Nietzsche's works provide an important window on the state of his contemporary reception in the Anglo-American world of philosophy. With the strong exception of Maude-marie Clark and Brian Leiter's essential introduction to their edition of *Daybreak* (translated by R. J. Hollingdale), the introductions by the other editors are merely better or worse exercises in apologetics.[1] These examples of largely "damning with faint praise" rhetoric follow a typical pattern of going on at length about all the ways that Nietzsche is not a philosopher in the traditional sense where that sense is defined by the narrowest of precedents in terms of temporal scope—at the earliest, since Kant, and usually since the rise of analytic philosophy in the last century—with the result that the rest of the introduction is taken up with arguing uphill whether Nietzsche's text can really be philosophy, and if so, how many nice insights it may be said to contain; or if not, what it might best be determined to be. Ralph Peter Horstmann, in his introduction to *Beyond Good and Evil*, gives a succinct version of this pattern of argument:

> There are quite a number of thinkers [presum-
> ably not in the Continental tradition] who

would insist that it makes no sense at all to at-
tribute greatness to any of Nietzsche's works. For
these readers, all of Nietzsche's writings are
flawed by serious shortcomings that justify fundamental complaints, ranging from accusations
that they are utterly irrational, or devoid of in-
formative content, to the conviction that they
contain nothing but silly proclamations based
on unwarranted generalizations—or a mixture
of both. According to proponents of this view,
the best way to think of Nietzsche's works is as
the disturbing documents of the creative process
of someone who was on the verge of madness.
To call any of his works great would therefore
amount to a categorical mistake. Interestingly
enough, this bleak evaluation is not based on
any disagreement with what the work's admirers
tell us we will find in it, or even any disagreement with the claim that it gives us the quintes-
sential Nietzsche.[2]

What turns this otherwise well-intentioned passage into an instance
supporting my argument is, of course, the last sentence here. If this
is really the case with Nietzsche—that there is no difference in what
his admirers and detractors find in his work—then we are not dealing with something that can be adjudicated by reasoned arguments,
but instead are dealing with a matter of individual taste (pace Kant).
Horstmann himself concludes as much when he adds that it is "a
perplexing fact that it is by no means easy to decide which of these
two conflicting attitudes towards [Nietzsche's work] should prevail,
and in the end it may be a rather personal matter."[3]

Whatever the weaknesses in Horstmann's introduction, he at
least goes on to attempt a recuperation, albeit weak, of Nietzsche's

insights in *Beyond Good and Evil*. Bernard Williams, an important philosopher in his own right as well as a great classicist in the Anglo-American tradition, leaves little of Nietzsche's skin after the following paragraph of his introduction to *The Gay Science:*

> Nietzsche's general reflections, here as elsewhere, have some recurrent weaknesses. There are cranky reflections on diet and climate. His opinions about women and sex, even if they include . . . one or two shrewd and compassionate insights into the conventions of his time, are often shallow and sometimes embarrassing; they were, biographically, the product of an experience which had been drastically limited and disappointing. However, what is most significant for his thought as a whole is the fact that his resources for thinking about modern society and politics, in particular about the modern state, were very thin. The point is not that he was opposed to a free society, equal rights, and other typically modern aspirations (though he certainly was . . .). In fact, Nietzsche has by no means been a hero exclusively of the political Right, and many radical, socialist and even feminist groups in the last century found support in his writings. This was possible just because the deeply radical spirit of his work was combined with a lack of effective political and social ideas, leaving a blank on which many different aspirations could be projected. His clearly aristocratic sympathies are, in political connections, not so much reactionary as archaic, and while he has many illuminating things to say about the religious and cultural history of

> Europe, his conception of social relations owes
> more to his understanding of the ancient world
> than to a grasp of modernity. The idea of nihilism
> which is so important in his later works is unde-
> niably relevant to modern conditions, but his
> discussions of such subjects as "corruption" . . .
> borrow a lot from the rhetoric of the Roman
> Empire and the disposition of its writers to
> praise the largely imaginary virtues of the van-
> ished Republic.[4]

Each time Williams commends Nietzsche, grudgingly to be sure, he proceeds to cancel out his own commendation. This ironic pattern, in the above paragraph, is strikingly evident, virtually sentence by sentence. Whatever apologetics Williams may be said then to engage in on Nietzsche's behalf are doomed to be overshadowed by these early remarks in this introduction.

Maudemarie Clark and Brian Leiter, in their introduction to *Daybreak*, place Nietzsche's views about morality in the context of Kant's and Schopenhauer's positions and his early naturalistic critique of them, a result of his reading in the contemporaneous literature of developments in modern physiology—what is often too simply termed German materialism—that is, the philosophy of Feuerbach and its influence on the scientific work and writings of Ludwig Buchner and Friedrich Lange. In other words, Clark and Leiter take seriously Nietzsche's views from the beginning of their introduction. They show how he critiques the picture of free will, "from a *naturalistic* view of persons as *determined* in their actions by the fundamental physiological and psychological facts about them," and thus they also show how Nietzsche reasonably concludes that "traditional morality," as summed up in his time, despite their differences, by Kant and Schopenhauer, must be "inhospitable to certain types of human flourishing" which arise most favorably in conditions like that of the ancient world (with its conception of nobility), where the illusion of free agency is not so dominant, as it is in modernity.[5] Clark and Leiter, focusing on section 103 in *Daybreak* ("There Are Two Kinds of Deniers of Morality"), further demonstrate that Nietzsche exemplifies both kinds of deniers in his work. He denies the claims of moral motivation by satirically pointing out the unmoral motivations underlying these often cynically offered claims, and he also denies the truth of genuine moral motivation as being based on false premises. Clark and Leiter see in *Daybreak* a major shift from a primarily satiric to a primarily substantive critique of modern morality.

They use as a guide to their reading of Nietzsche the following section in *Beyond Good and Evil:*

> Morality in the traditional sense, the morality of intentions, was a prejudice, precipitate and perhaps provisional—sometime on the order of astrology and alchemy . . . The decisive value of an action lies precisely in what is *unintentional* in it, while everything that is Intentional, everything about it that can be seen, known, "conscious," still belongs to its surface and skin—which, like every skin, betrays something but *conceals* even more.[6]

They find anticipations of this position in sections 115, 116, 119, 129, and 130 of *Daybreak*. While at times deploying analogically Kant's idea of the unknown thing-in-itself behind external appearance for the conscious mind's relationship to what lies beneath its surface, Nietzsche's above use of the metaphor of the body's skin makes clear that this unknown inner something both betrays itself as well as conceals itself.[7] Nietzsche's view is very much like the way psychoanalysis understands pathological symptoms in their semiotic relationship to the unconscious as signs to be deciphered, as "words" the old philologist in Nietzsche or in us can read. Thus, the true sources of human action are unconscious, largely unknown, and perhaps hardly knowable in themselves, but in their totality they are, for Nietzsche, as is the totality of external nature, unknowable in principle:

> However far a man may go in self-knowledge,
> nothing however can be more incomplete than
> his image of the totality of *drives* which consti-
> tute his being. He can scarcely name even the
> cruder ones: their number and strength, their
> ebb and flood, their play and counterplay among
> one another and above all the laws of their *nutri-*
> *ment* remain wholly unknown to him.[8]

Even when we consciously determine ourselves to combat one of the drives, we are likely to be in error as to what we are about and what is actually happening in us:

> *That one desires* to combat the vehemence of a
> drive at all, however, does not stand within our
> own power; nor does the choice of any particu-
> lar method; nor does the success or failure of
> this method. What is clearly the case is that in
> this entire procedure our intellect is only the
> blind instrument of *another drive* which is a *rival*
> of the drive whose vehemence is tormenting us:
> whether it be the drive to restfulness, or the fear
> of disgrace and other evil consequences, or love.
> While "we" believe we are complaining about
> the vehemence of a drive, at bottom it is one
> drive *which is complaining about another;* that is

> to say: for us to become aware that we are suffer-
> ing from the *vehemence* of a drive presupposes
> the existence of another equally vehement or
> even more vehement drive, and that a *struggle* is
> in prospect in which our intellect is going to
> have to take sides.[9]

Because of our human finitude as natural creatures, then, we are in no rational position to know and so to evaluate, to judge defini-tively, one way or another, the totality of existence, what Heideg-ger will remind us to call "Being." As such, nihilism, which assumes as correct its judgment that everything is meaningless and so de-serves to be destroyed, is not a perspective really supported by the facts of life.

As early as "On Truth and Lying in a Non-Moral Sense" (1873), Nietzsche takes this position and never wavers from it. As Pierre Klossowski in *Nietzsche and the Vicious Circle* (1969) and in his es-says on Nietzsche in *Such a Deathly Desire* (1963) demonstrates in detail, Nietzsche sees nerve stimuli, what in their more organized forms Nietzsche calls affects and drives, whether originating from external or internal sources, as the causes of a series of transposi-tions, transferences, and translations, from impulse to image (or phantasm) to acoustic sign (or word) to simulacrum (or concep-tual schema) to generic form (or category) to conventional cultural representation in the columbarium of dead metaphors which we call truth. But in fact, Nietzsche declares in "On Truth and Lying" that truth is a

> mobile army of metaphors, metonymies, anthro-
> pomorphisms, in short a sum of human rela-
> tions which have been subjected to poetic and
> rhetorical intensification, translation, and deco-
> ration, and which, after they have been in use

> for a long time, strike a people as firmly estab-
> lished, canonical, and binding; truths are illu-
> sions of which we have forgotten they are . . .
> metaphors which have become worn by frequent
> use and have lost all sensuous vigor.[10]

Deconstruction, as practiced by Derrida and Paul de Man and their followers, repeated the lesson of this early Nietzschean text. The recent history of Nietzsche's reception nonetheless appears to have largely forgotten all of this.

If we take Nietzsche seriously the way the deconstructionists once did and, to their credit, the way Maudemarie Clark and Brian Leiter do above (and to Keith Ansell-Pearson's no lesser credit in his introduction to the revised edition of the Cambridge *On the Genealogy of Morality*), then we can see how Nietzsche provides us with a broadly semiotic method of critical reading. Using it we can discover in our interpretive acts, and genealogically in other such acts in cultural history, more of the real truth about the always *potentially representative* struggle of our human, all-too-human drives than traditional philosophical ethics can ever do. Why should this self-critical possibility become a powerful motive force generally and at this time? A passage from *The Gay Science* that Klossowski typically makes much of in his work and Williams as typically ignores in his introduction gives the strongest answer to this question. I give the German word *Stimmung* in the following passage where appropriate to highlight the affective dimension of what Heidegger famously understands as "mood," as well as the conceptual connection to recent developments in contemporary philology, particularly the work of Hans Ulrich Gumbrecht, thereby, I hope, successfully suggesting the methodical scope of the issue involved when we speak of reading:

> *The "humanity" of the future.*—When I view this
> age with the eyes of a distant age, I can find

nothing odder in present-day man than his pe-
culiar virtue and disease called "the sense of history." This is the beginning of something
completely new and strange in history: if one
gave this seed a few more centuries and more, it
might ultimately become a wonderful growth
with an equally wonderful smell that could
make our old earth more agreeable to inhabit.
We present-day humans are just beginning to
form the chain of a very powerful future feeling
[*Stimmung*], link by link—we hardly know
what we are doing. It seems to us almost as if we
are dealing not with a new feeling [*Stimmung*]
but with a decrease in all old feelings [*Gefühlen*]:
the sense of history is still something so poor
and cold, and many are struck by it as by a frost
and made even poorer and colder by it. To others it appears as the sign of old age creeping up,
and they see our planet as a melancholy sick man
who chronicles his youth in order to forget his
present condition. Indeed, that is one colour of
this new feeling [*Gefühl*]: he who is able to feel
the history of man altogether as his own history
feels in a monstrous generalization all the grief
of his youth, thinking of health, of the old man
thinking of the dreams of his youth, of the lover
robbed of his beloved, of the martyr whose ideal
is perishing, of the hero on the eve after a battle
that decided nothing but brought him wounds
and the loss of a friend. But to bear and to be
able to bear this monstrous sum of all kinds of
grief and still be the hero who, on the second
day of battle, greets dawn and his fortune as a

person whose horizon stretches millennia before
and behind him, as the dutiful heir to all the nobility of past spirit, as the most aristocratic of
old nobles and at the same time the first of a
new nobility the likes of which no age has ever
seen or dreamt: to take this upon one's soul—
the oldest, newest, losses, hopes, conquests, vic-
tories of humanity. To finally take all this into
one soul and compress it into one feeling [*Stimmung*]—this would surely have to produce a
happiness unknown to humanity so far: a divine
happiness full of power and love, full of tears
and laughter, a happiness which, like the sun in
the evening, continually draws on its inex-
haustible riches, giving them away and pouring
them into the sea, a happiness which, like the
evening sun, feels richest when even the poorest
of fishermen is rowing with a golden oar! This
divine feeling [*Stimmung*] would then be
called—humanity![11]

This passage from book 4, "St. Januarius," of *The Gay Science* clearly
not only anticipates this future moment in human history, it also
anticipates the future moment of this very book when the reader
will confront Nietzsche's critique of "The Dying Socrates" (section
340) as a decadent who knew he was a decadent and so longed for
death; of "The Greatest Weight" (341) placed on us by the demonic
prospect of the eternal recurrence; and of "Incipit Tragoedia" (342),
essentially the opening passage of Nietzsche's next book, *Thus Spoke
Zarathustra,* in which the doctrines of the will-to-power, the self-
overcoming *Übermensch,* and the eternal recurrence are for the first
time explicitly coordinated.[12] The above section 337, "The 'Humanity' of the Future," I contend, implicitly brings together these

three doctrines in its performance of its prophetic vision. The figure of the sun and its generous total expenditure of energy that glorifies and transfigures with gold all things, even the humble fisherman and his oar, is a powerful image of self-overcoming worthy of the authentic Nietzschean superman and his ultimate refinement of the will-to-power into a divine feeling. As this prophecy makes clear, this feeling is a present event: an emerging aesthetic moment gathered into a linked chain of affect from all the past and projected as perpetually coming from and as the future of humanity.

Nietzsche's critique of the modern subject makes possible this exemplary performance of a new regulatory idea for an ethics of reading that can have more than merely textual impact (as "textual" is once again now commonly understood). As Nietzsche puts it in a February 11, 1883, letter to Franz Overbeck, his "physical style of thinking" is like "having an extra sense organ and a new, terrible source of suffering."[13] This is why in a letter (winter 1884–85) to Carl Fuchs, Nietzsche drones on and on—to his own admitted embarrassment—about the differences between ancient Greek accentual verse and modern rhythmic verse. The prolongation or shortening of temporal stress of classical Greek versus the mechanical filling out of simple beat-patterns (as he later also reiterates in letters to Peter Gast near the end of his working life) not only means the difference between a singing and spoken poetry, it also means the difference between two radically different experiences of time and of what it means to be human.[14] These are the high stakes of reading for Nietzsche.

A way to clarify further why this is so can be gained by comparing Nietzsche's position—his "physical style of thinking," philosophical semiotics of the drives, and ethics of the event of self-reading—to those of Lacan and Badiou. I choose them because they, like Nietzsche, stress the eventlike quality of experience, especially with respect to the discovery of truth.

Lacan's category of the Real and Badiou's concept of the truth-event and its subsequent procedures of fidelity, like Nietzsche's visionary reading as most fully represented in "the humanity of the future" passage just discussed, all depend upon a recognition of what Kurt Gödel in his famous "proofs" demonstrated definitively, namely, that any arithmetical system, formal structure, or even simple set of logically related elements—or, as Nietzsche would have it, a language or a text, say, or a morality or an entire culture—can never be both coherent and complete. There is always a "surd element" that is equally necessary and gratuitous with respect to the formal system in question. If the system is coherent, it has to be incomplete, and if it is incoherent, it will prove to be rather uselessly complete. Lacan calls this feature of systematic formalization the Real. It is the gap, abyss, or "black hole" in representation, where psychosis emerges. Badiou socializes this systematic gap in his notion of the state of the situation. This formal gap in the state of any situation is the disruptive force of what has been subtracted from the domain of politics, science, art, or love. It then may emerge as the event of a new truth bursting upon the world for which we invent procedures of rationalization and fidelity so as to test out this truth's authenticity and applicability, its universality, repeatedly over time. Nietzsche's doctrines of the will-to-power, of the self-overcoming *Übermensch,* and of the eternal recurrence of the same are his catachrestical figures for, respectively, the physics of this gap in systematic formation, its self-critical ethics, and its formative experience of time.

Armed with Nietzsche's method of self-reading, his "physical style of thinking," in which reading the body like reading a text can effect actual material transformations in the self and its world, we may once again validly claim for the humanities a significant cultural place in humanity's future.

3

Nietzsche's Passion in *The Gay Science:* An Experiment in Creative Reading

I begin by explaining my subtitle. By "an experiment in creative reading," I mean a reading of reading. This reading of reading is based upon Nietzsche's interpretive theory and practice. I call this Nietzsche's "speculative philology," in critical counterpoint to James I. Porter's view of Nietzschean hermeneutics, in *Nietzsche and the Philology of the Future,* which he designates "skeptical philology."[1] As I see Nietzsche's form of philology, it experimentally generalizes the condition of the reader to the point where it can serve as a model of the human condition per se, indeed at times as a model for how all beings act. In this way, via his largely future readers, Nietzsche tests the truth-value of his insight into what and how we know and don't know the world and ourselves, not by logic and the scientific method, but by imaginative surmise and creative intuition, and so how best we may live. Taking such an approach, I am of course indebted to the work of Sarah Kofman in *Nietzsche and Metaphor* and her groundbreaking analysis of what she calls "Nietzsche's uncategorizable text."[2]

Nietzsche's insight, to put it all too simply, is that we stand in relation to the world and ourselves having to translate what we perceive into figures of speech that have a largely unknown and unknowable relationship to their referents. As a result, we must perceive, think, and speak metaphorically. As Bernd Magnus puts it in his introduction to *The Cambridge Companion to Nietzsche*, we deploy "catachresis upon catachresis," even as convention and habit make us forget that we do so, to the point where we act as if we know the truth of things.[3] At best, what we can validly say is that, perhaps, we know something about ourselves and how we incorporate experience via the dark conceit, the allegorical mirror, of our uses of language. As a species, whose nature is still admittedly largely undetermined, we translate a nerve stimulus into an arbitrary image of the external world or of our inner state (or sometimes both at once, as in what we call a drive—this focus on the drives is what generally defines Nietzsche's "passion"). We then translate this image into a word, the word then into a concept, the concept into what becomes a customary truth, all the while automatically deleting and eliding differences according to the schematics of our minds, so that what we are left with at the end of this largely unconscious collective process is, Nietzsche reminds us, a well-worn coin whose face and back have virtually lost all trace of its human origins. We then exchange this truth, pragmatically and with a good conscience, in an economy of customary lying that we call telling the truth. In this context, in fact, the liar is the one who refuses to employ the customary usages, preferring instead his or her own newly minted inventions, or simply inverting the more lively commonplaces, often for selfish or hurtful purposes. It is worth recalling here Nietzsche's summation of truth as "illusions of which we have forgotten they are . . . metaphors which have become worn by frequent use and have lost all sensuous vigor"; that is, Nietzsche has a purely skeptical, nominalist view of truth.[4] Nietzsche never wavers from this basic position throughout all the changes in his short but volatile intellectual career.

This doesn't mean, however, that Nietzsche simply dismisses all our pretensions to knowledge out of hand—to do so would be dogmatic, after all, not truly skeptical, as Porter would remind us. Instead, he argues experimentally that this unconscious translation into human terms of ultimately unknown outer and inner worlds plays itself out in a passionate, even Hobbesian contest of drives, with each drive acting against all and all against each, so as to expend their ever-accumulating differential quantities of energy to the maximum level of discharge, thereby producing the greatest summation of release of tension, which most human beings call "pleasure," but Nietzsche calls "strength" or "power." For Nietzsche, every moment of existence, not just the first moment, is potentially a "big bang." Occasionally, of course, there is a truce or compromise-formation produced among drives; and rarest of all, sometimes one drive becomes dominant and for an extended period of time, perhaps even for a lifetime, such as the will-to-truth in the case of the philosopher, or the will-to-conquer in a Caesar. We can read this contest of drives, albeit speculatively, hypothetically, via the aesthetic and rhetorical effects—signs and symptoms—of the necessarily self-divided texts we make of our lives. Finding the textual hinges of their divisions opens any of these texts up, momentarily, to our often dazzled, horrified, or self-blinding gaze—or so, Nietzsche speculates, it would appear.

For instance, in section 339 ("Vita Femina") of *The Gay Science,* Nietzsche argues that given the fateful contingency of all things, sometimes it must be the case that unknowable outer and inner worlds of nature and human second nature "coincide" aesthetically in a "beautiful moment" of mutual unveiling:

> It requires the rarest of lucky accidents for the
> clouds that veil the peaks to lift for us momen-
> tarily and for the sun to shine on them. Not
> only must we stand in just the right spot to see
> this, but our own soul, too, must itself have
> pulled the veil from its heights and must have
> been in need of some external expression and
> parable, as if it needed a hold in order to retain

control of itself. But so rarely does all this coincide that I am inclined to believe that the highest peaks of everything good, be it work, deed, humanity, or nature, have so far remained hidden and covered from the majority and even from the best. But what does unveil itself for us *unveils itself for us only once!* . . . I mean to say that the world is brimming with beautiful things but nevertheless poor, very poor in beautiful moments and in the unveilings of those things. But perhaps that is the strongest magic of life: it is covered by a veil of beautiful possibilities, woven with threads of gold—promising, resisting, bashful, mocking, compassionate, and seductive. Yes, life is a woman![5]

Admittedly, Nietzsche's personification of life as a woman is sexist, but as such, so very traditional, customary. What is not traditional, however, and is more inventive, is that this image of woman unveiling herself represents, for him, the beautiful moment of at least apparently *mutual* unveiling of "subject" and "object," which means in the traditional sexist lingo he deploys here against itself, the masterful male-subject and passive female-object exhibit themselves, alike, as part of the parable to be provisionally read. Reading this beautiful moment using a well-known metaphor of life as a woman but in a critically revisionary way for a process or event he admittedly can only speculate about, Nietzsche is much like a blind philologist translating the insights of a long-dead language into his own version of Braille. In turn, we then have to translate him very carefully, with the right touch, or tact, but no less, I think, *speculatively,* that is, *experimentally,* open to all who would test out the reading experience for themselves. In any event, this is what I mean by both "speculative philology" and "an experiment in creative reading." And given the context of the "gay science," which alludes explicitly to the science of poetry of the troubadours, the Provençal poets whose lyrics are credited with inspiring the courtly love ethic and medieval romance narratives, Nietzsche's passion, as in the previously cited passage, takes on all the imaginative dimensions of a quest-romance incorporated into his reading experiments so as to structure his philosophical project. Given the pervasive presence of medieval romance representations in late nineteenth-century European high and more popular culture—everything from great philological works to the arts and crafts movement of William Morris and the Pre-Raphaelites to Wagner's repeated use of romance conventions in his operas and to the quest-romance structuring both anthropological approaches to ancient religions and contemporary military ideology, and so much more—it is not surprising that Nietzsche would make use of these late romantic themes and conventions for his own purposes.

To clarify this claim, we should return to Lacan's theory of the Real and Badiou's notion of the truth-event. As the event of new truth emerges in the world and we test out this eventful truth's authenticity and applicability, we do so knowing both that this will change the situation and that there must always be an unnamable element remaining in any new situation that we must never force our revisionary designation upon, or else we replicate the repressive dimension of the situation from which the new truth would release us. Nietzsche's "beautiful moments" are those in which the formless dimensions of the Real and the fugitive conditions of the truth-event can be read, albeit speculatively, experimentally, but nonetheless potentially by us all.

Before turning to a closer examination of *The Gay Science* and especially book 4, "St. Januarius," I must now differentiate Nietzsche from Lacan and Badiou. I agree with Babette E. Babich in "A Note on Nietzsche's *Chaos sive natura*" that unlike the rather abstract gap in formalized structures and systems, what Lacan calls the Real and

Badiou redescribes mathematically as the void or null-set of any set of elements, Nietzsche sees such a break in representation in terms of his classicist training as the original principle of Chaos and Old Night returning to irrupt into our world. As Harold Bloom has taught us, this irruption is the "surd element" in the literary practice of intertextual figural allusion. This Chaos is a mythic being combining the functions of both sexes but usually pictured as female, whose name means basically "chasm" or "gap," but not abstractly so. Rather, there is invested in this sense of Chaos all the passionate intensity of Orphic mysteries and the momentous historical transformations from matriarchy to patriarchy in the cultural history of the human species. Babich rightly traces Nietzsche's interest in this figure back to the myth of Zeus and Dionysus, twice-born, from Semele and from Zeus's thigh:

> For Nietzsche, what matters is not merely to pay
> homage . . . to the old story of the primordial
> goddess, or, with Goethe, to the literally named
> mothers of being. Instead, Nietzsche encourages
> us to attend to the powers of wild nature in cre-
> ative self-genesis, to shape oneself out of oneself
> and so to become oneself a work of art.[6]

The famous section 125, "The Madman," in *The Gay Science* that announces the death of God confirms how Nietzsche sees modernity as the time when the species faces a new and equally momentous transformation, from patriarchy to what new cultural system we still as yet know not.

This fraught historical perspective is key to understanding what is at stake in reading for Nietzsche. The God of tradition has underwritten not only the conventional values and premises of Western culture, a prospect which can sound distantly abstract at times; this God also has underwritten the sense of personal identity, the form of subjectivity, which language performs and supports, for nearly the last two millennia. Even if we do not subscribe to Lacan's theory of the paternal metaphor, wherein the name of the father acts to suture the person to a subject-position and thereby keeps the person as subject from sliding into psychosis, and has done so not just for two thousand years but since the beginning of civilization itself, we can see that the death of the traditional God can readily be experienced as a radical loss of given identity and a critical demand to quest for a new identity at all costs. With Nietzsche's view that language has produced and reinforced any given identity, to write and read without a model of identity means one has to attempt to write and to read not only creatively but also carefully. It is all too easy, it would seem, to lose one's head, like a latter-day Don Quixote, at the very least, and maybe become much worse off than that:

> God is dead! . . . And we have killed him! How can we console ourselves, the murderers of all murderers! The holiest and the mightiest thing the world has ever possessed has bled to death under our knives: who will wipe away this blood from us? With what water could we clean ourselves? What festivals of atonement, what holy games will we have to invent for ourselves? Is the magnitude of this deed not too great for us? Do we not ourselves have to become gods merely to appear worthy of it?[7]

What Nietzsche realizes is that in the coming age—our time—when the death of God, like the light of a distant star, finally reaches the mass of people, the resultant tremendous potential for sheer madness, the madness of thinking themselves gods and trying to act accordingly, will become pandemic as much in their political as in their personal lives.

As we know from section 108, "New Battles," however, even after knowledge that God is dead becomes universally available, the good fight against the lasting influence of God will have to be fought:

> After Buddha was dead, they still showed his
> shadow in a cave for centuries—a tremendous,
> gruesome shadow. God is dead; but given the
> way people are, there may still for millennia be
> caves in which they show his shadow.—And
> we—we must still defeat his shadow as well.[8]

What this means for Nietzsche is that in his texts, as here in *The Gay Science,* he must both go on offense against the shadow (or specter) of the dead God and discover a defense against the temptation to madness, especially the megalomaniacal regression that would enshrine oneself as a god. Nietzsche's solution to this dilemma in book 4, "St. Januarius," is ironically to entertain the feeling of liberation that the old God's death entails, itself a sublime, even divine feeling, literally awesome, as long-held emotional investments in the world return to the self; and to offer his select reader the prospect of his example in which he uses such newly released energies, no longer tied to the dead God's service, to transfigure the world, as the sun in the evening paints everything with its golden glow. Nietzsche would take away the guilt for God's murder from us, and replace it with an imaginative vision of the total *innocent* expenditure of creative power, on behalf of a literally brighter future for humanity. The quest for such a liberating identity defines more specifically Nietzsche's passion in book 4 of *The Gay Science.*

Jill Marsden in her fine article "The Art of the Aphorism" rightly reminds us that as "forms of eternity" or striking, apparently random verbal quanta of intensity and insight, Nietzsche's aphorisms resist being turned into logical arguments manqué or fragments of a grand narrative of any kind. I want to argue in the following demonstration, however, that in book 4, "St. Januarius," there is a narrative that the sections in this book allude to in their deliberately unsystematic and essayistic way.[9] As I have suggested, this overarching narrative is a modern version of the quest-romance, in which Nietzsche the poetic quester courts and espouses the "higher" powers of his own self, which have now been freed by the death of God, so as to turn these powers loose, not primarily in critical destruction, but in a creative expression of gratitude for his life, and to life generally. That this quest-romance ends at best ambiguously, as we will see, primarily means that there is more story to be told, that Nietzsche's exemplary "passion" goes on, not only for him, but even more so now for us.

One important sign that an overarching narrative deliberately, albeit delicately, informs the presentation of his aphorisms here is the solar imagery in "St. Januarius," which appears in fourteen of the sixty-six aphorisms, or roughly once every four to five intervals. Naturally, Nietzsche does not in fact insert these solar aphorisms into the book with the regularity of a metronome, but as we read and reread "St. Januarius" we come to expect their virtually musical refrain. Since Nietzsche sees *The Gay Science* as a "medial" work in every way, it punctuates, like a caesura, his intellectual career with major pronouncements—that God is dead, that a higher human type is possible, that the will-to-power is an incessant drive for self-overcoming of all things, that the eternal recurrence is both a horrific and enraptured vision defining his teaching—and book 4 performs these Nietzschean experimental truths in an imaginative style worthy of comparison with Dante's *Vita Nuova,* another text of prose and poetry about the rebirth of the man into the life of the poet. The solar imagery—a star in space amidst the chaotic labyrinth of the cosmos; the repeated rising and setting of the sun; the creation of a sun of one's own and the ability, like Walt Whitman's, to send it out of oneself each day according to one's own schedule of festivals and work; the power of the sun to transfigure, for a beautiful moment, all that it lights, even the ugliest of things, into golden images—these are just the major topoi that Nietzsche tropes upon in "St. Januarius." And as we know, Nietzsche's title refers not only to the Italian saint Gennaro, whose blood is supposedly kept in a vial and on feast days is said to run red again; it likely also refers to Janus, the Roman god of doors, entrances, and thresholds, whose two faces looking backward and forward remind us that the present moment is always potentially a critical transition, even as they may also recall the masks of tragedy and comedy, a mélange that Kathleen Marie Higgins attempts to address in *Comic Relief: Nietzsche's Gay Science*.[10] Nietzsche creates a context for his attentive readers to read the story of his passionate quest for identity as a critical lesson—perhaps exemplary, perhaps cautionary, and perhaps in a tragic-comic mode—for us all. That is, Nietzsche is both his own guinea pig and, potentially, depending on how we read him as he puts at risk his intellectual life, ours.

Nietzsche gives his reader a guide for reading him in book 4, in section 333, "What Knowing Means." He deconstructs Spinoza's famous remark originally made in Latin, that knowing is not ridiculing, or lamenting, or despising, but rather something else, even as it may combine elements of all three of these other acts. Instead of accepting this view, Nietzsche asks what is this knowing, "other than the way we become sensible of the other three."[11] He then continues his analysis by offering his alternative hypothesis that knowing is a "result of the different and conflicting impulses to laugh, lament, and curse."[12] There is a fight or contest between and among our unconscious drives, each one of which is an intense energy-quantum of one response or other. Sometimes, as a result of this largely unknown bodily contest, or agon, "a kind of justice and contract" result, what we would call, after Freud, a compromise-formation: "for in virtue of justice and a contract all these impulses can assert and maintain themselves in existence and each can finally feel it is in the right vis-à-vis all the others."[13] In this light, knowing is "*only a certain behaviour of the drives towards one another.*"[14] I would argue that we can substitute for the word "knowing" here that of "reading," for reading is an act of knowing that is the result of a contest of drives in, between, and among the writer, the text unconsciously expressing the drives, and the reader. "Indeed, there may be many hidden instances for *heroism* in our warring depths, but certainly nothing divine, eternally resting in itself, as Spinoza supposed."[15]

The experimental goal of this impulsive jousting or interpretative *psychomachia,* in book 4, is given antithetically in the parable of the lake in section 285. After asking who now has the strength to will "the eternal recurrence of war and peace," and so renounce the pleasures of a calm life of contemplation, Nietzsche recounts: "There is a lake that one day refused to let itself flow off and formed a dam where it used to flow off; ever since, this lake rises higher and higher. Perhaps this very renunciation will lend us the strength . . . perhaps man will rise ever higher when he no longer *flows off* into a god."[16]

Section 288, "High Spirits," presents the possible long-term psychophysiological consequences of the species becoming like this lake:

> It seems to me that most people simply do not
> believe in elevated moods, unless it be for mo-
> ments or fifteen minute intervals at most—ex-
> cept for those few who experience an elevated
> feeling over a longer period. But to be the
> human being of one elevated feeling, the em-
> bodiment of a single great mood, has hitherto
> been a mere dream and enchanting possibility;
> as yet, history does not offer us any certain ex-
> amples of it. Nevertheless history might one day
> beget such people too, given the creation and
> determination of a great many preconditions
> that even the dice rolls of the luckiest chance
> could not put together today. Perhaps the usual

> state for these souls would be what has so far en-
> tered our souls only as an occasional exception
> that made us shudder: a perpetual movement
> between high and low and the feeling of high
> and low; a continual sense of ascending stairs
> and at the same time of resting on clouds.[17]

The persons or people of the future who would be able to incarnate such a mood as described here, which reminds one of the musical scale in its heights and depths, and perhaps also is meant to be suggestive of something like the highly resonant Tristan chord of Wagner, would live their entire lives spontaneously feeling divine: "a continual sense of ascending stairs and at the same time of resting on clouds." This admittedly speculative hypothesis finds its basis in the literal sense of mood or *Stimmung*, which can mean being fully attuned, on the part of the self, to its situation in the world, something Heidegger will pick up on and elaborate fully in *Being and Time* (1927).

What motive informs this vision of the future? For that answer we need to return to the opening sections of book 4, where Nietzsche first introduces himself as the good modern philosopher following in Descartes' footsteps; and then notes his situation of thinking and living again after almost dying. He next warns himself (and us) against believing, as Goethe does at the opening of *Dichtung und Wahrheit,* that one has a personal providence guiding one's life, like a good star or genius, demon or guardian angel. The third of these opening sections (section 278), "The Thought of Death," now gives us a possible motive for using our human, all-too-human interpretive power, which Nietzsche has just praised and demystified in speaking about the superstitious idea of a personal providence, for more magnanimous purposes:

> It gives me a melancholy happiness to live in the
> midst of this jumble of lanes, needs, and voices:

how much enjoyment, impatience, desire; how much thirsty life and drunkenness of life comes to light every moment of the day! And yet things will soon be so silent for all these noisy, living, life-thirsty ones! How even now everyone's shadow stands behind him, as his dark fellow traveller! It's always like the last moment before the departures of an emigrant ship: people have more say to each other than ever; the hour is late; the ocean and its desolate silence await impatiently behind all the noise—so covetous, so certain of its prey. And everyone, everyone takes the past to be little or nothing while the near future is everything: hence this haste, this clamour, this outshouting and outhustling one another. Everyone wants to be the first in this future—and yet death and deathly silence are the only things certain and common to all in this future! How strange that this sole certainty and commonality barely makes an impression on people and that they are *farthest* removed from feeling like a brotherhood of death! It makes me happy to see that people do not at all want to think the thought of death! I would very much like to do something that would make the thought of life even a hundred times more *worth being thought* to them.[18]

This passage strikes one as not being what most people think of when they hear Nietzsche's name, but I would argue that it is in fact the key to understanding his design in book 4 of *The Gay Science* and his philosophical mission more generally; which is, I believe, so to transfigure everyday life, as Nietzsche does here, making

it a fit subject for his strikingly poetic prose; that is, so to take back
into oneself the projections of millennia, once exhausted in the service of the old God and now set loose; and to use those newly released and potentially destructive energies for an aesthetic justification
of life; for in this way we all may one day embrace *amor fati* as pas-
sionately as he does. This passion for bestowing his passion for life,
despite all counterarguments, especially suffering, is Nietzsche's
motive that shapes his experiments in creative reading throughout
his career, but is most beautifully realized in such passages as this
one from "St. Januarius."

We receive confirmation that this is Nietzsche's motive from
section 289, "Get on the Ships." This section lays out pretty fully
Nietzsche's vision for the modern philosopher, even correcting di-
alectically any impression from section 279 that pity might unwit-
tingly inform his project in an ultimate way:

> If one considers how an overall philosophical
> justification of one's way of living and thinking
> affects each individual—namely, like a sun,
> warming, blessing, impregnating, shining espe-
> cially for him; how it makes him independent of
> praise and blame, self-sufficient, rich, generous
> with happiness and good will; how it incessantly
> turns evil into good, brings all forces to bloom
> and ripen and keeps the petty, great weed of
> melancholy and moroseness from coming up at
> all—one exclaims longingly, in the end: Oh,
> how I wish that many such new suns would yet
> be created! Even the evil man, the unhappy
> man, and the exceptional man should have their
> philosophy, their good right, their sunshine! Pity
> for them is not what is needed! We have to un-
> learn this arrogant notion, however long hu-

manity has spent learning and practicing it—we
do not need to present them with confessors,
conjurers of souls, and forgivers of sins; rather, a
new *justice* is needed! And a new motto! And
new philosophers! The moral earth, too, is
round. The moral earth, too, has antipodes! The
antipodes, too, have their right to exist! There is
another world to discover—and more than one!
On to the ships, you philosophers![19]

Section 290, "One Thing Is Needful," follows, and we are to understand that, for Nietzsche, giving style to oneself and being one
of these Odysseus-like philosopher-poets, who inspire us by their
examples to create our own suns, are one and the same thing, as
they will thereby envision a new justice for the moral earth, with all
its diverse beings. The subject of the future is at once a work of art
to be put together out of mixed raw materials and a planetary being,
like Wallace Stevens's "Planet on the Table," his famous late poem
about the publication of his collected poetry.

As Nietzsche tells us above in section 333 on Spinoza and
"What Knowing Means," however; or underscores at length in section 335, "Long Live Physics"; or, as David Allison reminds us in
Reading the New Nietzsche, more playfully and poetically in section
310, "Will and Wave," expresses his secret identity with the waves;
any conscious presentation of intention is only half the story, at
best, a compromise formation among the drives.[20] So what is going
on below the surface of these passages, what largely unconscious
psychomachia? I think we can make a strongly plausible hypothesis
by turning to this book's final sections on the dying Socrates, the
demon of the eternal recurrence, and the beginning of the tragedy
of Zarathustra, but first we must briefly revisit "Vita Femina."

Traditionally in quest-romance, whether in its simplified allegorical narrative of knights, dragons, and ladies fair, or in what

Northrop Frye and Harold Bloom famously identified as its romantic internalized form of psychosexual struggle for identity, there must be a confrontation between the hero and the femme fatale, what Blake in his internalized prophetic romances called "The Female Will," the demonic muse-figure. The former must definitively reject the latter, usually by unveiling her and exposing the evil monster underneath the alluring mask, who must then be slain, thereby releasing the old king and his virtuous daughter and their land from the curse of infertility afflicting it. We can easily recall for examples one or another medieval romance, Spenser's *Faerie Queene,* or any of the internalized Oedipal quests of Wordsworth, Shelley, or Keats. The curse in internalized romance is the lack of creativity, the evil monster is whatever blocks creativity, and redemption is what then frees creativity from its ensnarement by this evil. Both my book *The Romance of Interpretation: Visionary Criticism from Pater to de Man* (1985) and Jean-Pierre Mileur's *The Critical Romance: The Critic as Reader, Writer, Hero* (1990) explore and critique the presence of romance in modern and contemporary criticism.[21]

In "Vita Femina" (section 339), we recall, Nietzsche stages less an unveiling than a recognition scene, reversing traditional expectations along these lines, celebrating the infinite folds of seductive appearances, and a mutual but partial unveiling of hero and witch (or femme fatale); in other words, a fuller acceptance and affirmation of the quest's infinite nature: "But perhaps that is the strongest magic of life: it is covered by a veil of beautiful possibilities, woven with threads of gold—promising, resisting, bashful, mocking, compassionate, and seductive. Yes, life is a woman!"[22] Since it is Nietzsche's genius to realize that it is the old morality itself and its cultural forms, including traditional quest-romance, that is the true monster blocking human creativity, then it is altogether ironically fitting, if at times comically hilarious or tragically lamentable, that the romantic internalized quest become a quest to overcome itself and its origins.

Similarly, in section 340, "The Dying Socrates," Nietzsche turns the tables on the old king of philosophy, and says why after all he is really a seducer to decadence that must be overcome:

> I admire the courage and wisdom of Socrates in everything he did, said—and did not say. This mocking, love-sick monster and pied piper of Athens, who made the most audacious youths of Athens tremble and sob, was not only the wisest chatterer of all time; he was equally great in silence. I wish he had remained silent also in the last moments of his life—perhaps he would then belong to a still higher order of minds. Whether it was death or the poison or piety or malice—something loosened his tongue and he said: "O Crito, I owe Asclepius a rooster." This ridiculous and terrible "last word" means for those who have ears: "O Crito, *life is a disease.*" Is it possible that a man like him, who had lived cheerfully and like a soldier in plain view of everyone, was a pessimist? He had merely kept a cheerful demeanor while all his life hiding his ultimate judgment, his inmost feeling! Socrates, Socrates *suffered from life*! And then he still avenged himself—with this veiled, gruesome, pious, and blasphemous saying. Did a Socrates really need *revenge*? Was there one ounce too little magnanimity in his overabundant virtue?—O friends! We must overcome even the Greeks![23]

We see here Nietzsche's own internalized quest-romance, as we recall his New Year's resolution from the opening of book 4, section 276, "For the New Year":

> I want to learn more and more how to see what
> is necessary in things as what is beautiful in
> them—thus I will be one of those who make
> things beautiful. *Amor fati:* let that be my love
> from now on! I do not want to wage war against
> ugliness. I do not want to accuse; I do not even
> want to accuse the accusers. Let *looking away* be
> my only negation! And, all in all and on the
> whole: some day I want only to be a Yes-sayer![24]

Similarly, just as he warns us in section 277, "Personal Providence,"
against a Goethean trust in one's guiding star or demon, since it is
actually our own interpretive power to turn every "apparent" failure in life into a real success; so, too, this warning is mirrored by
what is probably the most famous single passage in book 4, section
341, "The Heaviest Weight." Nietzsche presents explicitly here for
the first time his doctrine of the eternal recurrence of the same as
the vision of his demon. This vision is a test, a questioning not only
of his own powers of interpretation—is this vision the greatest opportunity for nihilistic despair and negation or grateful affirmation
and joy?—but of his and our will-to-power to overcome ourselves
because we love life more than anything else and can practice a
heroic magnanimity making for the future of humanity, indeed,
perhaps making for a future super-humanity:

> What if some day or night a demon were to steal
> into your loneliest loneliness and say to you: "The
> life as you now live it and have lived it you will
> have to live once again and innumerable times
> more; and there will be nothing new in it, but
> every pain and every joy and every thought and
> sigh and everything unspeakably small or great in
> your life must return to you, all in the same suc-

cession and sequence—even this spider and this moonlight between the trees, and even this moment and I myself. The eternal hourglass of existence is turned over again and again, and you with it, speck of dust!" Would you not throw yourself down and gnash your teeth and curse the demon who spoke thus? Or have you once experienced a tremendous moment when you would have answered him: "You are a god, and never have I heard anything more divine." If this thought gained power over you, as you are it would transform and possibly crush you; the question in each and every thing, "Do you want this again and innumerable times again?" would lie on your actions as the heaviest weight! Or how well disposed would you have to become to yourself and to life *to long for nothing more fervently* than for this ultimate eternal confirmation and seal?[25]

Nietzsche leaves the identity of the demon ironically open, but whether we think of Socrates' demon, Goethe's personal and/or Faust's traditional demons, or the great demon Eros, what one does with one's creative will, now that it is released from its service to the old god, lies behind this passage, as well as, of course, Nietzsche's own personal suffering from his childhood on. This vision is the hardest test for Nietzsche or any of us to overcome. We must sublimate our will-to-power into a will-to-love. Nietzsche reminds us in section 334 that we must learn to do so, and so be able to transfigure existence into what section 337 calls "The 'Humanity' of the Future." Such a philosophical project, if generally practiced, will ensure an affirmative future for humanity:

To finally take all this [history of human experi-

ence] into one soul and compress it into one
feeling—this would surely have to produce a
happiness unknown to humanity so far: a divine
happiness full of power and love, full of tears
and laughter, a happiness which, like the sun in
the evening, continually draws on its inex-
haustible riches, giving them away and pouring
them into the sea, a happiness which, like the
evening sun, feels richest when even the poorest
of fishermen is rowing with a golden oar! This
divine feeling would then be called—humanity![26]

Since the beginning and the end of "St. Januarius" in *The Gay
Science* dovetail nicely with each other here, we can now read the
middle sections of this book as doing two things: first, demonstrating the obstacles to and blockages of the creative will, all those
things Nietzsche and all moderns have to overcome in our world
and ourselves; and second, displaying the linkages of signs and figures, as in the case of the solar imagery symbolizing magnanimous
imaginative expenditure, which stitch together this text. Finally, as
we read the last section (342), "Incipit Tragoedia," we understand
that Nietzsche's passion is for a tragic romance—that includes its
own parodic satyr play, in which all the experiences of the species,
its highs and lows, its madness and its genius, would be compressed
into one soul and personified by one figure, a tragic-comic cultural
icon of a new justice for our moral, still all-too-moral planet that
would not also be in the end merely another hollow idol:

When Zarathustra was thirty years old, he left
his homeland and Lake Urmi and went into the
mountains. There he enjoyed his spirit and soli-
tude, and did not tire of that for ten years. But
at last his heart changed—and one morning he

48

arose with rosy dawn, stepped before the sun,
and spoke to it thus: "You great heavenly body!
What would your happiness be if you did not
have those for whom you shine! For ten years
you have climbed up to my cave; without me,
my eagle, and my snake, you would have become tired of your light and of this road; but we
awaited you every morning, relieved you of your
overabundance, and blessed you for it. Behold, I
am sick of my wisdom, like a bee that has collected too much honey; I need outstretched
hands; I would like to give away and distribute
until the wise among humans once again enjoy
their folly and the poor once again their riches.
For that I must step into the depths, as you do
in the evening when you go behind the sea and
bring light even to the underworld, you over-
rich heavenly body! Like you I must *go under,* as
it is called by the human beings to whom I want
to descend. So bless me then, you calm eye that
can look without envy upon all-too-great happiness! Bless the cup that wants to overflow in
order that the water may flow golden from it
and everywhere carry the reflection of your bliss!
Behold, this cup wants to become empty again,
and Zarathustra wants to become human again."
Thus began Zarathustra's going under.[27]

All the major themes and tropes of book 4 converge here and are
synthesized in the beginning of Zarathustra's story, which in its
more literary mode would repeat, as we know, the major ideas and
discursive prose formulations in *The Gay Science* once again. This
formal elaboration creates the prospect of an aesthetic principle for

a life of imaginative self-experimentation for Nietzsche and for those who follow after him, a prospect and a principle which are potentially endless. This textual play constitutes Nietzsche's passion of creative reading and, perhaps, ours:

> You will also want to help—but only those whose distress you properly *understand* because they share with you one suffering and one hope— your *friends*—and only in the way you help yourself: I want to make them braver, more persevering, simpler, more full of gaiety. I want to teach them what is today understood by so few, least of all by the preachers of compassion [*Mitleiden*]: to share not pain, but *joy* [*Mitfreude*]![28]

Any reader then may access the real of such a critical interpretation's truth-event.

What I have hoped to do in this "experiment in creative reading," then, is to interpret Nietzsche's career from its medial point, *The Gay Science,* and especially the pivotal point of book 4, "St. Januarius," which looks backward and forward, as I have tried to suggest, so self-consciously in many ways. Before this text are Nietzsche's juvenilia and first distinctive works in something like his own voice; after this text, there is *Zarathustra* and the great nay-saying works to all those things that block our creativity now that he has found his principle of affirmation for life which can overcome these blockages. *Ecce Homo,* the final work of virtual madness, would then reveal the ironically joyful masks of the gods at their tragic war with each other, those gods who he thinks will ultimately decide the future of humanity in our new, modern, albeit increasingly polytheistic epoch, with each subject his or her own god—Dionysus versus The Crucified, perhaps, but only at the very least.

4

Nietzsche's Book for All and None: The Singularity of *Thus Spoke Zarathustra*

When I decided to write on Nietzsche's *Thus Spoke Zarathustra: A Book for All and None,* I was surprised to discover that there were six English translations currently in print, in addition to a convenient German paperback version of *Also sprach Zarathustra: Ein Buch für Alle und Keinen* in the standard Giorgio Colli and Mazzino Montinari edition.[1] For many years, there were only two English translations readily available, those of Walter Kaufmann and R. J. Hollingdale.[2] Then, beginning in 1997, which saw the Wordsworth Classics reprint of the 1908 English translation by Thomas Common (ed. Nicholas Davey), three newly translated editions followed: two in 2005, by Barnes and Noble Classics (trans. Clancy Martin and ed. Kathleen M. Higgins and Robert C. Solomon) and Oxford World Classics (trans. and ed. Graham Parkes), and the latest in 2006, in the Cambridge Texts in the History of Philosophy series (trans. Adrian Del Caro and ed. Adrian Del Caro and Robert Pippin).[3]

Having immersed myself in these translations for a while and in the German original for comparison, which I will cite at times herein, as well as the Cambridge edition, I have decided that they all have their merits, but none of them have captured the original's singularity. Of course, any sophisticated translator knows that this must be so in the case of any work of translation. However, I mean by my judgment that *Thus Spoke Zarathustra* raises the question of any kind of translation in a profound way. The original German text is not only resistant to translation into another language just as any text resists translation due to the recognizable differences between two languages; it is untranslatable just the way one cannot really translate a proper name from its original tongue into another without often self-defeating hilarity. That is, just as we would not dream of translating "Friedrich Nietzsche" into English by making it "Fred Niche," so, too, every effort to translate any aspect of the original text leads to the failure to determine it definitively. In saying this, I realize that we do translate names from one language to another; for example, Zoroaster is a translation from Persian originally into Greek, and so Zarathustra is a translation into German of this name. But such translations, even after centuries, still sound funny to native speakers of the languages involved. The translations call attention to themselves as inadequate representations of a singularity—not so much hard, resistant grit in the machine as gaps in its functional operations.

There has been considerable work done on both the idea of the proper name and that of singularity. Peggy Kamuf in *Signatures: The Institution of Authorship,* Brian Greene in *The Elegant Universe,* and Ray Kurzweil in *The Singularity Is Near,* among others, have written accessibly on singularity in the linguistic, cosmological, and technological domains. So, too, in *Proper Names* has Emmanuel Levinas written about it, in ethics. Often, when writing about singularity, whatever the context, there is an aura of the sublime and a sense of triumph over what I call the culture of representation—basically, modern post-Enlightenment culture that would reduce all differences to measurable, calculable, and marketable ones, under the global hegemony of late capitalism. But in *Zarathustra,* singularity is a problem, not a solution.

After repeatedly asking his disciples or representatives of the people who and what they think he is, Zarathustra then names himself repeatedly this or that—as the prophet of the overman in book 1, as the discoverer of the self-overcoming of the will-to-power in all things in book 2, and most definitively, it appears, as the teacher of the eternal recurrence of the same in book 3. But then the satyr play of book 4 puts into ironic, self-parodic question all and any definitions, nominations, or christenings, including especially self-definitions. The reader begins to reread this text, whose genre is still open fittingly to endless arguments, convinced that it has, perhaps, fooled him or her into misreading the meaning, intention, style, and tone, and when comparing English to German texts, this suspicion of the reader only grows exponentially with each rereading. Unlike Napoleon, who named and crowned himself emperor, Zarathustra, like Nietzsche, neither has a definitive symbolic identity given to him, nor does he rest content with the identity he makes for himself. Instead, at best, Zarathustra adopts this or the lineaments of a symbolic identity that only the future, he hopes, will fill in.

Having lost his identity as the original founder of the moral system whose own morality of truthfulness has now been undermined conclusively, Zarathustra, while being the first to recognize this fate, as Nietzsche says in *Ecce Homo,* is left without any positive identity. This situation is the modern fate: as the old god has died, the symbolic function of the father has become increasingly eclipsed by this death, and all of us have to create identities for ourselves. Given that no one model or measure, no norm of identity is acceptable to all, often group identities of some sort substitute their paradigms. But *Zarathustra* hollows out in advance, with critique and irony, any and all possible substitutes for traditional identity—such as nationality, gender, sexual orientation, class, and so on—insofar as they buy into the culture of representation; that is, insofar as they do not insist on their singular differences from the reductive metaphoric and conceptual compromise-formations that would formulate, in the words of William Blake, "one law for the ox and the lion," which he, like Nietzsche after him, saw as a form of "tyranny" over the creative will.

Unfortunately, however, being a writer or a philosopher with no positive identity incorporated into the system of representation of your culture, at whatever level—that of family, social group, religion, profession, nation-state, or civilization—means that one is like the mad person who possesses and is possessed by a private language. In saying this, I do not mean to suggest anything about Nietzsche's own psychological state during the time of writing *Zarathustra,* or later. What I want to highlight is that Nietzsche writes *Zarathustra* precisely to produce a singular text that yet presents his singular identity. Imagine an experiment that results in a black hole suddenly appearing in everyday life: such is the effect of the event of this text. We can never forget it, nor, no matter how many times we read and study it, can we accommodate its laws— or "chaos"—to the laws of the culture of representation. We remain faithful to the experience that *Zarathustra* was for Nietzsche and is for his attentive reader by then focusing in our experimental readings of it on the problem of identity it singularly exhibits.

Zarathustra is aware of the difficulty of the impossible quest for a singular identity. In "The Bestowing Virtue" ("Von der schenkenden Tugend") in part 1, he remarks famously, "Not only the reason of millennia—their madness too breaks out in us. It is dangerous to be an heir."[4] "Nicht nur die Vernunft von Jahrtausenden—auch ihr Wahnsinn bricht an uns aus. Gefährlich ist es, Erbe zu sein."[5] One of the major issues facing Zarathustra, like that of modernity itself, is how to incorporate the identity of the inherited past, including his own role in that past, while simultaneously breaking with it and so making a radically new identity of the future possible. Even as Zarathustra claims that his disciples, like him, thirst to become sacrifices for and gifts to posterity, by compelling "all things to and into yourself, so that they may gush back from your well as the gifts of your love," how to bestow these gifts is a question that defines who one is.[6] We will see how for Zarathustra this question of incorporation, how one does it, becomes definitive for framing the question of his identity.

Of course, "Who is Nietzsche's Zarathustra?" is a question that, at least since Heidegger asked it originally in 1953, has informed Nietzsche studies.[7] Everyone, from Heidegger himself to Georges Bataille, Jacques Derrida, Michel Foucault, Sarah Kofman, Paul de Man, and David Allison, among many other Nietzschean philosophers and scholars, has attempted to answer this question.[8] And Lawrence Lampert in *Nietzsche's Teaching,* Stanley Rosen in *The Mask of Enlightenment,* and T. K. Seung in *Nietzsche's Epic of the Soul* have devoted their book-long analyses of the text to saying just who Zarathustra is: the prophetic teacher of the eternal recurrence, the transparent mask of the radical nihilist who tragically failed to overcome his own nihilism, and the heroic protagonist of a modern epic of the human soul's self-redemption.[9] The difference in my approach is that I do not attempt to answer the identity-question raised by *Zarathustra* or by Nietzsche and his work as a whole. Instead, I propose to lay out its problematic formulation in this central text. Three key scenes in *Zarathustra* play out the problem of identity in the important context of self-erasing representability: "On Redemption" ("Von der Erlösung") and "On the Vision and the Riddle" ("Von Gesicht und Räthsel") in part 2, and "The Convalescent" ("Der Genesende") in part 3. The final section in part 4, "The Sign" ("Das Zeichen"), then adds a formally ironic, and so unresolved, "closing" to the problem of identity, one that returns us to the problematic of identity and cultural inheritance that appears in part 1 of *Zarathustra.* Whatever else the eternal recurrence of the same may be or refer to, the hermeneutic circle, as it structures this text, is surely one of the best candidates for understanding it.

"Von der Erlösung" is a title that could be translated equally well by "deliverance," perhaps even "release." An unbinding is suggested, but from what? The first part of this chapter tells us. Crossing over the bridge from the Blessed Isles (the home of the dead?), Zarathustra encounters a number of "the cripples and the beggars."[10] A hunchback steps forward and demands that Zarathustra convince him and the other cripples and beggars of his message. The hunchback wants Zarathustra to perform miracles, removing his hump, for instance, but Zarathustra responds by saying that it is precisely his hump that gives any hunchback spirit. Similarly, with other possible candidates for miracles—the blind, the lame, and so on—once they are healed they would regret the change because they would have lost their opportunity for self-overcoming, being left instead with opportunities for the worse.

Zarathustra further responds by declaring that there is something far worse than a cripple, namely, what he calls "an inverse cripple," "ein umgekehrter Krüppel."[11] Human beings, throughout history, lie in ruins, as on a battlefield or a butcher-field. Not so much from war, as from specialization, in which the good of the whole body is sacrificed to the specialization of one function or talent. Zarathustra tells of seeing a giant ear attached to a tiny stalk of a body, with a bloated boil of a soul and a tiny envious face, and being told this person is a musical genius. That is, in addition to those born crippled or disabled in some way, and those made so by war and natural disasters, there are the inverse cripples whose cultivated talents and chosen roles have truncated their humanity. If he were left only with the past and present, Zarathustra would despair, "a cripple at the bridge," but he is "a seer, a willer, a creator, a future himself and a bridge to the future," and so he can envision a larger whole to come.[12] But who is this Zarathustra?

> And you too asked yourselves often: "Who is
> Zarathustra to us? How shall he be known to
> us?" And like me you gave yourselves questions

for answers. Is he a promiser? Or a fulfiller? A
conqueror? Or an inheritor? An autumn? Or
a plow? A physician? Or a convalescent? Is
he a poet? Or a truthful man? A liberator?
Or a tamer? A good man? Or an evil man?[13]

Zarathustra answers by his action: "I walk among human beings as
among the fragments of the future; that future that I see." "Ich
wandle unter Menschen als den Bruchstücken der Zukunft: jener
Zukunft, die ich schaue."[14] "And all my creating and striving
amounts to this, that I create and piece together into one, what is
now fragment and riddle and grisly accident . . . To redeem those
who are the past and to recreate all 'it was' into 'thus I willed it!'—
only that would I call redemption!"[15]

Because the human will cannot will backward and change the
past, it suffers in silence at the spectacle of disaster that is the past
and because "the spirit of revenge" would expend its blocked and
bound energies on acts of vengeance against others and oneself.[16]
The only redemption, then, the only deliverance and unbinding,
is for the creative will to learn to will backward and realize, "All 'it
was' is a fragment, a riddle, a grisly accident" until it says: " 'But I
will it thus! I shall will it thus!' "[17] Zarathustra would become the
teacher of the self-overcoming creative will in this regard.

Here we see how Zarathustra envisions the relationship between the will-to-power and the overman. The overman is the
human being who has learned the lesson of how to will backward
and transform fragment, riddle, and grisly accident into a new future whole. By accepting and incorporating the past, personal and
world historical, the self-overcoming will can redeem the uncanny
fragments and distortions of humanity by re-creating and placing
them in an original totality.

The problem with this vision of the creative will is that, while
grand, it is hardly specific, and further, as this chapter ends, the

hunchback notices that Zarathustra has a moment of apparent shock, as if appalled at his own vision, but says nothing. He asks Zarathustra why he fails to speak his mind not only to the people but to his own disciples, but Zarathustra remains silent. Part of this is surely for dramatic effect, as Zarathustra will fully reveal his doctrine of the eternal recurrence of the same in part 3 of *Thus Spoke Zarathustra,* in the "On the Vision and the Riddle" chapter. But I also think that there is inherently a problem with this vision of the creative will redeeming the past by learning to will backward and so freeing itself from the spirit of revenge. First of all, such willing backward sounds like nothing more than the usual belated rationalization everyone practices. Surely, that is not what Zarathustra has in mind, given his dramatic pronouncements? Secondly, how can the will both accept the past and transform it? Such a double-bind intention is schizoid, like attempting to remember to forget. Finally, if we anticipate the doctrine of the eternal recurrence of the same that will be completely unveiled soon, then we are confronting a situation in which we must reconcile how it is that all that was will return exactly as it has been, to all eternity, with the will's imperative to revise the past. For if the human past is fundamentally fragmentary, enigmatic, and grisly, then how can its eternal recurrence as the same in the entire circle of time work to change anything, and so free the will from the spirit of revenge that would deny time and "its it was" with all its schemes of vengeance against others and oneself?

"On the Vision and the Riddle," the second chapter of part 3 of *Zarathustra,* may help to address these questions. Like the other scenes I am focusing on here, it is one of the narrative portions of the text, which includes Zarathustra declaiming, not just one of his speeches standing alone. As such, it works more like a novel or an allegorical discourse than like an oration, which means as literary critics we can feel readier to analyze it.

The chapter begins with Zarathustra leaving his Blessed Isle and traveling over the bridge to the mainland to the port where ships embark for distant lands. Once aboard ship, he hides out for a while, but when he emerges he addresses the sailors and tells them the story of "the vision and the riddle." One night, in despair and having just recovered from an illness, Zarathustra climbs up a mountain path accompanied by his arch-enemy, "the spirit of gravity," who is described as part dwarf, part mole. This weird, grotesque creature immediately tells us we are in a mythic landscape where anything may happen, as in folk tales, romantic allegories, or Wagner's operas.

As Zarathustra pauses at a gateway to confront his enemy—"Dwarf—you or I"—as if to finally have it out with him, Zarathustra prepares to announce his "most abysmal thought," "meinen abgründlichen Gedanken."[18] Zarathustra declares that this gateway is called "Moment," and here two paths cross and contradict each other, that of the eternal past and that of the eternal future, all that was and all that will be. In asking the dwarf his opinion on the question of whether these two pathways must contradict each other, the dwarf answers mockingly, with a singsong parody of the eternal recurrence of the same: " 'All that is straight lies,' murmured the dwarf contemptuously. 'All truth is crooked, time itself is a circle.' "[19] Zarathustra tells the dwarf not to make things too easy for himself with such facile parody. He then fully reveals the vision of the eternal recurrence:

> "See this moment!" I continued. "From this gateway Moment a long eternal lane stretches *backward:* behind us lies an eternity. Must not whatever *can* happen, already have happened, been done, passed by before? And if everything has already been here before, what do you think of this moment, dwarf? Must this gateway too not already—have been here? And are not all

59

> things firmly knotted together in such a way
> that this moment draws after it *all* things to
> come? Therefore—itself as well? For whatever
> *can* run, even in this long lane *outward—must*
> run it once more!" "Denn, was laufen kann
> von allen Dingen: auch in dieser langen Gasse
> hinaus—muss es einmal noch laufen!"[20]

No sooner does Zarathustra disclose his most abysmal thought, that even the most mundane or creepy details of the present moment, the spinning spider, the eerie moonlight, all will return eternally, than suddenly he hears a dog howl nearby.

As his thoughts race back to his childhood for the last time he heard a dog howling like this that inspired his pity so much, Zarathustra feels as if he has woken from a dream—or perhaps into one, as the landscape completely changes because what he saw then he now sees again:

> "Then I heard a dog howl like this. And I saw it
> too, bristling, its head up, trembling in the
> stillest midnight when even dogs believe in
> ghosts: so that I felt pity: For the full moon had
> passed over the house, silent as death, and it
> had just stopped, a round smolder—stopped on
> the flat roof just as if on a stranger's property—
> that is why the dog was so horror-stricken, be-
> cause as folklore has it, dogs believe in thieves
> and ghosts. And when I heard it howl like this
> again, I felt pity once more. Where now was the
> dwarf? And the gateway? And the spider? And
> all the whispering? Was I dreaming? Was I wak-
> ing? I stood all of a sudden among wild cliffs,
> alone, desolate, in the most desolate moonlight.

But there lay a human being! And there! The dog
jumping, bristling, whining—now it saw me
coming—then it howled again, it *screamed:* had
I ever heard a dog scream like this for help?"²¹

The German for the "scream" and "screamed" is, respectively, *schrei*
and *schrein,* which primarily means "cry" and is used in construc-
tions that in English would give us "crybaby" and the like; that is,
"cry," as in a baby crying, would probably be the better translation
here. In fact, R. J. Hollingdale in note 21 to his translation of
Zarathustra claims the following, apparently relevant biographical
connection to this scene:

> This scene is a memory from Nietzsche's child-
> hood. Nietzsche's father died following a fall, and
> it seems that Nietzsche was attracted to the scene
> by the frightened barking of a dog: he found his
> father lying unconscious. It is not entirely clear
> why this scene should have been evoked at this
> point. The most likely suggestion is that Nietz-
> sche at one time thought that events recurred
> within historical time, and was troubled by the
> idea that he might meet the same death as his fa-
> ther. (The idea seems to have assumed the nature
> of an obsession: its origin probably lay in Nietz-
> sche's fear of madness, which was strengthened
> by the fact that his father died insane. The insan-
> ity was caused by the fall, but Nietzsche was
> probably doubtful whether the fall did not
> merely bring to the surface an inherited weak-
> ness.) This old idea may have come into the au-
> thor's mind at this point, and have been included
> in the text as a cryptic "history" of the theory of

the eternal recurrence. What follows [in the
scene] is symbolic and not actual.[22]

Nietzsche's father did die a few days after a fall from his horse, and
he was found at the site of the fall in part due to the howling of a
dog. The cause of his death was listed as "softening of the brain,"
apparently caused by the fall. Although Hollingdale confidently
claims Nietzsche discovered his father, no other commentator on
this scene does. David Farrell Krell, in "Consultations with the Paternal Shadow: Gasché, Derrida, and Klossowski on *Ecce Homo*,"
never discusses this scene of Nietzsche's father's death, but he does
analyze Nietzsche's two reports, from ages twelve and seventeen, of
his father's ghost rising from the grave and taking his brother, two-
year-old Joseph, back with him, to the accompaniment of haunting organ music.[23] Nonetheless, the cause of death given as
"softening of the brain" certainly suggests, among other things, the
final phase of syphilitic infection, general paralysis of the insane,
when the brain tissue actually rots, causing an irreversible spiral
into madness and death. We probably also cannot help but recall
Nietzsche's climactic breakdown in Turin into madness, when he
threw his arms around a horse to protect it from being beaten by
the driver of a cart. What I think is pertinent in Hollingdale's claim
is that the scene is clearly meant to exemplify something important
about the eternal recurrence of the same. Nietzsche probably never
believed that in anyone's lifetime things returned, unlike what
Hollingdale speculates, but there is ample evidence that he did believe that he reached the nadir of his bad health at the same age as
his father died. He may have thought that he inherited the same
arc of physiological decline, certainly not an unreasonable belief,
especially in the context of the time.

To see more clearly how this scene plays a key role in em-
bodying the enigmatic vision of the eternal recurrence of the same,
we now have to read the rest of it:

And truly, I saw something the like of which I
had never seen before. A young shepherd I saw;
writhing, choking, twitching, his face distorted,
with a thick black snake hanging from his
mouth. Had I ever seen so much nausea and
pale dread in one face? Surely I must have fallen
asleep? Then the snake crawled into his
throat—where it bit down firmly. My hand tore
at the snake and tore—in vain! It could not tear
the snake from his throat. Then it cried out of
me: "Bite down, Bite down! Bite off its head!
Bite down!"—Thus it cried out of me, my
dread, my hatred, my nausea, my pity, all my
good and bad cried out of me with one shout.[24]

Here are the last two sentences of the German: "Da schrie es aus
mir: 'Beiss zu! Beiss zu! Den Kopf ab! Beiss zu!—so schrie es aus mir,
mein Grauen, mein Hass, mein Ekel, mein Erbarmen, all mein
Gutes und Schlimmes schrie mit Einem Schrei aus mir."[25] While
Schlimmes is indeed "bad" and not "evil," as other translators render
it, such as Kaufmann, *schrie* here as verb and noun, which means
"cry" as in outcry or baby's cry, and not primarily "shout," "scream,"
or "shriek," should be read consistently as I have suggested.

Strangely, Zarathustra and apparently Nietzsche, and presumably the reader get so caught up in this scene that not only
where we are but when we are is not clear. By rereading and carefully attending to the temporal transitions, I think there are several
moments to be critically discriminated. First, there is the moment
of the telling, Zarathustra aboard ship telling his story to the
sailors, and to whom he is about to ask his riddle. Then, within the
story Zarathustra is telling, there is his account of the dwarf/mole,
the spirit of gravity, his arch-enemy, and the vision of the gateway
Moment. In the twinkling of an eye, there is an abrupt change in

scene, and the dwarf, the gateway, and the mountain landscape vanish, leaving Zarathustra confronting the sound of a howling dog. Next, we return to Zarathustra's (and perhaps Nietzsche's) childhood for a scene of the last time a howling dog made him feel pity as he does now in his newly changed scene. This childhood scene plays itself out in two parts—the first part is that of the house and the moon and the dog crying. But the second part is that of the young shepherd and the snake and Zarathustra's efforts to tear the snake from the shepherd's throat and his final cry, echoing the dog's, to bite the snake's head off. This second part—does it belong to the time of childhood and that howling dog, or does it belong to the time immediately following the dwarf's and the gateway's disappearance and the latest dog howling? If we say to childhood, then we have to imagine the young boy Zarathustra trying to tear the snake out of the shepherd's throat, and we risk a comic collapse into bathos. But if we say it belongs to the narrative moment immediately following the vision of the gateway and the dwarf, then we are in a dreamscape, a phantasmagoria without known coordinates in the spatial and temporal world of everyday life, something supported by Zarathustra's own confusion over where and when he is.

If we decide not to decide this question, à la a deconstructive reading, what we have then is a narrative moment, a most fantastical one at that, embedded within other, more linearly and literally discernible narrative moments: that is, we have the stylized simulacra of Zarathustra's remembered "actualities" and remembered "fantasies," his waking and/or dream-visions; and if we add into this heady mix, any of Hollingdale's biographical speculation, we end up holding in ironic suspension, in suspended judgment, in the way of absolute romantic irony, all these radical alternatives that threaten to explode at the slightest glancing touch.

Let us complete our reading of this last scene within the scenes by moving with Zarathustra into his sudden, final address to the sailors:

You bold ones around me! You searchers, re-
searchers and whoever among you ever shipped
out with cunning sails onto unexplored seas! You
riddle-happy ones! Now guess me this riddle
that I saw back then, now interpret me this vision of the loneliest one! For it was a vision and
a foreseeing: *what* did I see then as a parable?
And *who* is it that must some day come? *Who* is
the shepherd into whose throat everything that
is heaviest, blackest will crawl?—Meanwhile the
shepherd bit down as my shout [*shrie:* cry] ad-
vised him; he bit with a good bite! Far away he
spat the head of the snake—and he leaped to his
feet.—No longer a shepherd, no longer
human—a transformed, illuminated, *laughing*
being! Never yet on earth had I heard a human
being laugh as *he* laughed! Oh my brothers, I
heard a laughter that was no human laughter—
and now a thirst gnaws at me, a longing that
will never be still. My longing for this laughter
gnaws at me; oh how can I bear to go on living!
And how could I bear to die now![26]

Here is the German again for a part of this quotation, as the original in this case has at once a greater spiritual and material resonance
than any of the English translations: "Nicht mehr Hirt, nicht mehr
Mensch,—ein Verwandelter, ein Umleuchteter, welcher lachte!"[27] I
would translate this as "No longer shepherd, no longer human, a
transfigured, radiant being": the suggestion is at once of both an
angelic and a resurrected body, perhaps even of the pre-natural body
of Adam before the Fall. The word *Verwandelter* is used to refer to
the spiritual process of transubstantiation, as well as to physical
processes, such as ossification, calcification; what matters is that

the things—spiritual or physical—become transparent, illuminated, if you will, but as if by their own inner light shining forth radiantly, even smokily, like *ein Umleuchteter* or "wet room lamp." This resurrected shepherd, in other words, is not only laughing and shining, he is smoking hot! Like a new star, perhaps?

Be that as it may, what have we learned about the self-overcoming will-to-power of the future overman as he faces the vision and the riddle of the eternal recurrence of the same, as Zarathustra has step-by-step formulated it in this singular book for all and none?

I think we are at the core of what makes Nietzsche's text untranslatable. As we have seen, this chapter contains in suspension multiple temporal layers that in the final analysis do not explicate neatly; in fact, in addition to those we mentioned already, Zarathustra adds another temporal layer in his riddle to the sailors, that of the future coming of he who will laugh like the shepherd and so on. Clearly, too, this chapter is rife with phallic implications and ripe for psychoanalytic interpretations, of which Sara Kofman in *Explosion I* and *II*, for one commentator, has offered quite a few.[28] Whether we look at it in terms of Freud's vision of the Oedipus complex, Lacan's model of psychosis, or Kristeva's revision of narcissism and abjection—or of any other psychoanalytic theory, or for that matter, in terms of Christian pastoral associations or more broadly, anthropological visions of dying gods and the like—this text provides us with a rich mine. I prefer to read it in terms of Badiou's theory of the truth-event and truth-procedures. I take my permission to do so from the spirit of gravity, who in his contemptuous dwarf-like murmuring reminds us that "all truth is crooked, time itself is a circle," "Alles Gerade lügt, murmelte verächtlich der Zwerg. Alle Wahrheit ist krumm, die Zeit selber ist ein Kreis."[29] The word *krumm* also means "twisted" and "awry," as being out of joint, dislocated. The echoes of Shakespeare's *Hamlet* in this chapter are many. What I propose is that we see the eternal recurrence of the same as a vision of truth as event in the play of madness that marks the temporality of modernity.

We require now a slight detour back into Badiou's theory, specifically here into Badiou's ontology, before returning to a fuller reading of "On the Vision and the Riddle."

For Badiou, ontology is mathematics. That is, Being consists of infinite multiples upon multiples without end but without any One or order, except for what we axiomatically impose on it when we construct a set. Badiou, like Nietzsche, thus begins with the proposition that Being (Nature for Nietzsche) is spontaneously in itself, so far as we can say at all, a chaos, and that any order is an intentionally created one that, for Nietzsche, we often forget is such. Badiou is more explicit in seeing Being as a chaos of possible, fragmentary orders to be formulated by us into one order, on the analogy with set theory, according to the truth-events that occur to produce knowledge validated by the procedures we invent to confirm that knowledge. Politics, art, science, and love are the domains in which new truths arise. Philosophy is the domain where they are critically reflected upon and coordinated. The French Revolution, the invention of symphonic form, Einstein's theory of relativity, and the courtly love ethic are examples for Badiou of truth-events. The procedures we invent to remain faithful to them define the revisionary work of human institutions.

Because Being always appears for us in a situation, Badiou considers any situation a set of presented elements which are selected by the state of the situation. The state of the situation is the count that tells us what counts and does not count, what is an element and what is a member of any situation or set. Whether the set in question is that of all red objects in this room or something loftier, the state of the situation and its count separate the red objects from the others, making them members of the set where the others are elements presented by it but not represented in it. The null-set of any set founds it so that it does not end up in a potentially infinite regress in answer to the question: Is the set of all red objects in this room also a red object? If it is, then it is included in itself. If it is not, then it is excluded from itself, even as it must be included by definition. The null-set of a set is the founding void that prevents this sort of thing from happening. Whatever does not belong as a member to the set but is only an element of it or is even only potentially so, as in the case of the above question, is consigned to the void and is not part of the official repertoire or representation (or encyclopedia of knowledge) for this set.

Truth in any situation is the event in which something from the void emerges for a subject in that situation, and for Badiou a subject is always at least two, never just one, which is always a belated construction after the fact. For things we generally think of as individual pursuits, such as lyric poetry, say, Badiou sees the two of the human subject in the poet-reader relationship. The truth in question that emerges has no name, does not fit in the encyclopedia of knowledge; the repertoire of representation cannot readily accommodate the unnamable, the untranslatable. This does not mean that the state of the situation does not attempt to name it, to force it into the culture of representation and conventional knowledge, but one of the ways we can recognize the truth is that it resists such violent accommodation by what it is and by the subject it calls into existence via the truth-procedures people develop to do so. Such procedures would include new representations that the subject of this truth understands are by definition inadequate for the purpose of incorporating the truth into the system of representation. The truth-event is like something that we ingest but cannot digest or metabolize. "On the Vision and the Riddle" is for *Zarathustra,* as *Zarathustra* is for Nietzsche's corpus, and what Nietzsche is for us: the unincorporated, the un-incorporate-able. What the enigmatic atemporal vision of the choking and then laughing, transfigured shepherd is for Zarathustra, Nietzsche and this text are for us: the unnamable founding void of the modern subject—that which cannot be generally incorporated, but only specifically, indeed singularly, encrypted as such. What Kurt Gödel found to be the case for every and any system of distinguishable elements, that it is either incomplete or inconsistent due to the absence or presence of a surd element, is what Nietzsche's *Zarathustra* is for the now global modern system of representation.

"The Convalescent" chapter, near the end of part 3, dramatizes this truth. First of all, Zarathustra jumps up from his bed like a madman and berates for not yet being awake the impression his own body left on the bed, as if it were another person there. He then identifies, for his favorite animals, the eagle and the serpent (emblems of pride and wisdom), who the young shepherd is that he foresaw and saved in his enigmatic vision by counseling to "bite, bite"—himself, of course. So whether we follow Hollingdale in his biographical speculation or C. G. Jung and Ned Lukacher in their different archetypal readings of the figure of the Ouroboros, the snake with the tail in its mouth, as a symbol of eternity, we see that Zarathustra knows it all comes back to himself, even as his favorite animals remind him of his doctrine of the eternal recurrence: "In every Instant being begins; around every Here rolls the ball There. The middle is everywhere. Crooked is the path of eternity"; "In jedem Nu beginnt das Sein; um jedes Hier rollt sich die Kugel Dort. Die Mitte ist überall. Krumm ist der Pfad der Ewigkeit."[30] While *Die Mitte* can mean either "the middle" or "the center," given the long history in philosophy and theology of the idea of God being the center of the circle or sphere of Being that is everywhere, "center" would seem to be the better choice here, since Nietzsche redistributes the attributes of divinity to the details of everyday and not-so-everyday life.

Combining this vision with the scenario of the young shepherd, we can see that each moment is potentially a crisis of will. It requires a decision that we must creatively cut or bite through. We thereby will that this new, necessarily unknown moment to us be part of the eternal recurrence of the same, and we do so according to the principle of selection each of us is. As the vision of the young shepherd suggests, this principle is the ultimate fact and fate of us, that bit of largely unknown, unknowable, and irremediable nature that our encysted, atemporal, primal scenes encrypt in us.

Zarathustra responds to the mouthing of his doctrine by his favorite animals now:

> "Oh you foolish rascals and barrel organs!" an-
> swered Zarathustra, smiling again. "How well
> you know what had to come true in seven days
> [of his sickness]—and how that monster
> crawled into my throat and choked me! But I
> bit off its head and spat it away from me . . .
> My great surfeit of human beings—*that* choked
> me and crawled into my throat; and what the
> soothsayer said: 'All is the same, nothing is
> worth it, knowledge chokes . . . Eternally he re-
> turns, the human of whom you are weary, the
> small human being'—thus my sadness yawned
> and dragged its foot and could not fall asleep."[31]

Eventually, his favorite animals convince him to "sing and foam over," "Singe und brause über," and fashion a new poetic lyre for himself to do so.[32] Because he has "unfolded" his "ultimate depth," his "most abysmal thought," to "the light," so that his "abyss *speaks,*" Zarathustra must recognize and accept that "the knot of causes" in which he is entangled recurs, re-creating him and the small human being all over again and yet again.[33] By accepting this aspect of his vision, Zarathustra ends his down-going, and "as proclaimer" of the eternal recurrence of the same, he can now "perish!"[34] He may then be said to have earned his self-nomination: "I, Zarathustra, the advocate of life, the advocate of suffering, the advocate of the circle."[35] Of course, this self-nomination is purely poetic, untranslatable into any existing repertoire of conventional knowledge. Paradoxically enough, what defines the modern subject as such is just this singularity. With the spread of modernity across the planet, it is no wonder that traditional societies are resistant to, not to say radically in revolt against, this spread.

"The Sign," the last chapter in the fourth and final part of *Zarathustra*, replays this entire process of self-nominating identity, often in an ironic mode, including the renewed recognition of the danger of pity and self-pity, with respect to "the great cry of distress" that not just humanity as a whole but its supposedly highest specimens so far give off symptomatically, including Zarathustra, at the prospect of the eternal recurrence of the same. Zarathustra understands it as "my last sin," "meiner letsten Sünde."[36] As his lion scares away the higher men with whom he has celebrated the night before a drunken "Ass Festival," he suddenly senses that what he calls his children are nearby (presumably, the works he is to produce). Zarathustra then rejects pity for the pursuit of his work: "Ich trachte nach meinem Werke!"[37] The words *trachten nach* can mean to strive for, but also to covet, to woo, to aspire to, and such similar passionate acts. The highly parodic, indeed radically self-parodic scene thus ends on this serious note— with the event of Zarathustra's truth as indicated by the emergence of a new star in the constellation of human history: "Also sprach Zarathustra und verliese seine Höhle, glühend und stark, wie eine Morgensonne, die aus dunklen Bergen kommt," "Thus spoke Zarathustra and he left his cave, glowing and strong, like a morning sun that emerges from dark mountains."[38]

Of course, given the untranslatability of this event into anything other than what those procedures of reading experiments such as mine would remain faithful to, repeatedly, what this final scene says about who or what Zarathustra, or Nietzsche, or any of us is must remain an open question.

5

Ecce Homo: Nietzsche's Two Natures

After recently completing a book manuscript on the competing log-
ics of American visionary experience, I was invited to do an essay
on the ten volumes in the series Cambridge Texts in the History of
Philosophy that are devoted to Nietzsche's work.[1] I began my career,
thirty years ago, as a critical theorist influenced by Nietzsche's work
and that of his deconstructive interpreters. My first book, for instance, based on my dissertation, was *Tragic Knowledge: Yeats's Autobiography and Hermeneutics* (1981). I edited a special issue of
boundary 2 with leading Nietzscheans as contributors in this same
year, which was later published as *Why Nietzsche Now?* (1985).

Since that time, however, I have focused more on the institu-
tionalization of critical theory in the American academy, for better
and worse, than on the course of Nietzsche or other author studies.
In doing the essay on the Cambridge Nietzsche, I discovered that,
while interesting translations of Nietzsche's corpus informed by the
latest textual scholarship were being made available, the corpus itself was being treated as if the demonstrated necessity for close reading of his texts had never happened. The result of this critical
amnesia was that the editors' and translators' introductions to their
own chosen works were too often nothing more than pathetic exercises in apologetics, damning with faint praise or self-defeating

admissions that Nietzsche committed every illogical "sin" in the book, even inventing new ones, perhaps, along the way. They would then desperately attempt (and naturally fail) to salvage something of Nietzsche's reputation for Anglo-American academic philosophy. In short, the deconstructive literary Nietzsche was long dead and buried.

Given the general triumph of critical approaches oriented by the new historicist-informed identity politics in the present-day humanities, such a development is not really surprising, however unfortunate it may be from my critical perspective. What follows is one of the five chapters I have now written on Nietzsche's texts, reading them closely in light of this history of changing critical perspectives. The following analysis of *Ecce Homo,* a book that is still the best introduction to Nietzsche, is therefore a deliberate, and I hope, somewhat provocative, but finally and most of all, instructive experiment in reading that not only can have a practical bearing on the future of Nietzsche studies, but on that of the humanities more broadly.

I am struck in reading this autobiography again by the split that haunts it. This split is put on prominent display in the chapters "Why I Am So Clever" (section 9) and "Why I Write Such Good Books" (section 3 of Nietzsche's remarks on *Thus Spoke Zarathustra*), but a complete analysis would find it replicated everywhere in the text. The perspective Nietzsche adopts on his life remains broadly naturalistic; that is, within the domain of nature as generally and conflictingly understood in the late nineteenth century, at once as inorganic and mechanistic and as organic and living. These conflicting, even contradictory, positivist and romantic versions of nature shape fully the story of the life being narrated.

Nietzsche is clearly aware of this split, as his riddle opening the text underscores: "As my father I am already dead, as my mother I am still alive and growing old."[2] He is, in short, a decadent descending into the inorganic realm, even worse, a spectral apparition of the patriarchal voice, and a new beginning anticipating with the "great health" derived from his mother the triumph of life in overcoming itself once again by producing the new human type, perhaps the superhuman type.

The first memorable way this split appears occurs when Nietzsche speaks of "the whole casuistry of egoism."[3] The original German has *Selbstsucht* for "egoism" here, and may also be (and has been) translated correctly as "selfishness."[4] I will now cite the salient passages from section 9 of "Why I Am So Clever" on this topic, as it turns out that becoming what one is depends on "the whole casuistry of egoism":

> At this point I can no longer avoid giving the actual answer to the question of *how to become what you are.* And with this I touch on the master-stroke in the art of self-preservation—of *egoism* . . . For if you assume that your task, your destiny, the *fate* of your task lies considerably beyond the average measure, then no danger would be greater than facing up to yourself *with* this task. Becoming what you are presupposes that you have the slightest inkling *what* you are. From this point of view even life's *mistakes* have their own sense and value, the temporary byways and detours, the delays, the "modesties," the seriousness wasted on tasks which lie beyond *the* task. Here a great ruse, even the highest ruse can be expressed: where *nosce te ipsum* would be the recipe for decline, then forgetting yourself, *misunderstanding* yourself, belittling, constricting, mediocritizing yourself becomes good sense itself . . . You need to keep the whole surface of consciousness—consciousness *is* a surface—untainted by any of the great imperatives . . . Meanwhile, in

the depths, the organizing "idea" with a calling
to be master grows and grows—it begins to
command, it slowly leads you *back* out of by-
ways and detours, it prepares *individual* qualities
and skills which will one day prove indispens-
able as means to the whole—it trains one by one
all the *ancillary* capacities before it breathes a
word about the dominant task, about "goal,"
"purpose," "sense."—Seen from this angle my
life is simply miraculous.[5]

Duncan Large here takes some liberties with italics where Nietzsche in the original uses scare quotes or nothing at all, allowing
most often the rhythm of his German to give the stress or beat. But
basically, what comes through is that an entirely mechanical practice of unconscious self-defense and repression of the sort Freud
would try to lift from the burdened psyches of his neurotic patients
is exactly the kind of thing that works perfectly, Nietzsche claims,
when like him, one has a task as great as his revaluation of all values. Nietzsche allows that appearing selfless, even being so at times,
may be in the highest interests of "*egoism*" and "*self-discipline.*"[6] Yet,
the way the dominant "idea" operates, both in the passage above
and in the one to follow below, is like the way poetic inspiration is
said to work by romantic poets and theorists, whether Coleridge
or Schiller. Such inspiration also works unconsciously, but it does
so organically, creating spontaneously a unified whole where there
once was only at best a defensive and artificial hierarchy of psychic
powers held apart or compartmentalized and in suspension, not to
say, suspense:

The task of *revaluing values* required perhaps
more capacities than have ever dwelt together in
one individual, above all contradictory capacities,

too, without them being allowed to disturb or de-
stroy one another. Hierarchy of capacities; distance; the art of separating without creating
enemies; not conflating, not "reconciling" anything; an immense multiplicity which is nevertheless the opposite of chaos—this was the
precondition, the long, secret labour and artistry
of my instinct. Its *higher concern* was so pro-
nounced that I never even suspected what was
growing within me—that all my abilities would
one day suddenly *spring forth* ripe, in their ultimate perfection.[7]

Here is the German of this last crucial sentence: "Seine höhere
Obhut zeigte sich in dem Maasse stark, dass ich in keinem Falle
auch nur geahnt habe, was in mire wächst,—dass alle meine
Fähighkeiten plötzlich, reif, in ihrer letzten Vollkommenkeit eines
Tags hervorsprangen."[8] The imagery of this last sentence partakes of
the male parturition metaphor that dominates Nietzsche's discussion of *Thus Spoke Zarathustra*.

The highly artificial but original idea of order of rank among
his psychic powers, which the self-defense of "the whole casuistry
of egoism" produces, now gives way suddenly, *both piecemeal and all
at once,* to the spontaneous organic vision of this new birth of the
dominant and totalizing idea of his life-work, the revaluation of all
values. That is, the individual psychological representation of the
revaluation of all values in his life—the in- or un-organic order of
rank among his many conflicting powers—gives way to the romantic idealism of a new birth of apparently organic unity—except that this new birth is precisely composed of such revaluations
of all values as "the whole casuistry of egoism" being better than
Christian or any kind of moralistic selflessness, thereby poking a
stick in the eye of any would-be idealism.

This catachrestical birth-imagery recalls how the fraternal union of Apollo and Dionysus in *The Birth of Tragedy* produced Attic tragedy, or how Athena, like Sin in Milton's *Paradise Lost,* popped out of the head of Zeus, or maybe even how Zeus played surrogate "mother" to Dionysus in another one of the mythic tales. Perhaps the *Alien* movies, where the monstrous offspring leap from their human victims' abdomens, may also help to stress the paradoxical, not to say potentially self-parodic, nature of this surprising figurative and conceptual development. The image of the dominant "idea" with all its ancillary powers suddenly *springing forth* cannot help but recall both nature in springtime and, given that this idea and its powers are also ripe, in their ultimate perfection, the opening riddle of *Ecce Homo* in which Nietzsche says of himself that he is both a decadent and a new beginning. Nietzsche's vision here is one metaphor piled atop another, catachresis atop catachresis, with a vengeance.

Section 3 of the *Zarathustra* part of "Why I Write Such Good Books" adds to the sense of paradoxical and possibly parodic self-divided figuration. Nietzsche makes some of his most extravagant literary claims here:

> Does anyone at the end of the nineteenth cen-
> tury have a clear idea of what poets in strong
> ages called *inspiration*? If not, then I'll describe
> it.—With the slightest scrap of superstition in
> you, you would scarcely be able to dismiss the
> sense of being just an incarnation, just a mouth-
> piece, just a medium for powering forces. The
> notion of revelation—in the sense that suddenly,
> with ineffable assuredness and subtlety, some-
> thing becomes *visible,* audible, something that
> shakes you to the core and bowls you over—
> provides a simple description of the facts of the

matter. You hear, you don't search; you take, you don't ask who is giving; like a flash of lightning a thought flares up, with necessity, with no hesitation as to form—I never had any choice. A rapture whose immense tension is released from time to time in a flood of tears, when you cannot help your step running on one moment and slowing down the next; a perfect being-outside yourself with the most distinct consciousness of myriad subtle shudders and shivers right down to your toes; a depth of happiness where the most painful and sinister things act not as opposites but as determined, as induced, as a *necessary* colour within such a surfeit of light; an instinct for rhythmic conditions that spans wide spaces of forms—length, the need for a rhythm with a *wide span* is practically the measure of the power of the inspiration, a kind of compensation for its pressure and tension . . . Everything happens to the highest degree involuntarily, but as if in a rush of feeling free, of unconditionality, of power, of divinity . . . The involuntariness of images and analogies is the most remarkable thing; you lose your sense of what is an image, what an analogy; everything offers itself as the nearest, most correct, most straightforward expression. It really seems—to recall a phrase of Zarathustra's—as though the things themselves were stepping forward and offering themselves for allegorical purposes . . . This is *my* experience of inspiration; I have no doubt that you need to go back millennia in order to find someone who can say to me "it is mine, too."[9]

Before we write off Nietzsche's vision of inspiration as unwitting male hysteria, we must recall that he begins his discussion of *Zarathustra* with a preemptive joke at his own expense along such lines, that of a male fictional pregnancy, which sounds even funnier in German: "Diese Zahl gerade von achtzehn Monaten dürfte den Gedanken nahelegen, unter Buddhisten wenigstens, dass ich im Grunde ein Elephanten-Weibchen bin."[10] And finally, in the next two sections Nietzsche claims that, respectably, such literary inspiration makes the body dance involuntarily, like music, and it produces what he names "the *rancune* [rancor] of the great," that the great work or deed turns against the one who has been the breeding ground for it, via its terrible expenditure of energies leading to dangerous exhaustion and the specter of its greatness dogging one's subsequent life at every turn.[11] In this way, the split in *Ecce Homo* continues and deepens. We can see clearly this self-division between a romantic organic vision of his own nature (inspired and dancing) and a self-defensive allegorical vision of death, as if the specter of the rancor of the great haunting one were a form of negative magic to ward off the evil eye of his future readers by saying, "Look, I've suffered for this involuntary creative freedom, so don't begrudge me my achievement in *Zarathustra*." The reactive nature of the work produced belies the active nature of the worker—and vice versa.

What does this figurative, narrative, and conceptual contradiction between the inorganic and organic visions of order signify for Nietzsche's autobiography, for his work and philosophy, and for ourselves? Two ideas of structure are in conflict here: the spatialized hierarchy of a highly artificial and mechanical order of rank and the temporal progression of a spontaneous organic development, the neoclassical model of static representation and the Enlightenment model of progressive representation, which Foucault's early work analyzes so memorably and demonstrates definitively how this opposition at times is a hard-and-fast binary one and at others a permeable space of emergence. The "gap," "gulf," or "abyss" between these two models, as embodied in this text, in Nietzsche's corpus and career, and in contemporary discursive and textual modes, is also an affective matter.

Even in contemporary astrophysics and astronomy, we can see this. In "The End of Cosmology?" for instance, Lawrence M. Krause and Robert J. Scherrer, two leading figures in the field, argue that recent discoveries, such as that of the cosmological constant—that unlike what the Big Bang theory predicts, the universe is expanding at a faster and faster rate—give us two radically different visions of cosmic order.[12] The Big Bang theory suggests that after the universe runs out of gas, it will collapse in on itself and blow up all over again, in a surprising, albeit partial, confirmation of Nietzsche's idea of the eternal recurrence (here only the larger pattern repeats, not the details); while the cosmological constant theory—an idea of Einstein's that he once regretted sharing—suggests that the universe will continue expanding forever, with local galaxies clumping together into super-galaxies, such as the Andromeda Galaxy merging with us, and distant galaxies disappearing over the event-horizon of the visible universe's ultimate black hole at greater-than-light speeds, leaving the enlarged Milky Way in a sea of blackness until it is its turn to go. The infamously problematic dark matter and dark energy, they speculate, may be the trace residue of all the cosmic objects that have already so disappeared. Clearly, the lineaments of the two visions of nature haunting *Ecce Homo* are playing themselves out here.

In any event, the "void" that opens up, repeatedly and dizzyingly, in Nietzsche's *Ecce Homo* cannot help but resound with the prophetic echoes of his imminent collapse into madness—for instance, as he lashes out, briefly enraged, at his mother and sister: "to think of myself as related to such *canaille* [riffraff, rabble] would be to blaspheme against my divinity [*mein Göttlichkeit*]."[13] This could also be translated, without strain, as "my godliness," or "my godhood." I suppose that Nietzsche's self-staged apotheosis is one, admittedly "mad," way of mediating the chasms in his influential life-work.

Of course, this may be what *Ecce Homo* mostly tells us. That in a time when "God is dead" and so the paternal metaphor, as Lacan would say, no longer functions effectively to suture the conflicting, indeed contradictory, parts of the subject together, one solution to this modern plight is to put into the vacated gap of the now-vanished divine mediator and its avatars another idol, and who better than oneself? I think "Wie man wird, was man ist," might best be considered a self-help manual for would-be gods, or at least *Übermenschen*. Christie McDonald in "Sarah Kofman: Effecting Self Translation" argues that Kofman in her definitive two-volume study of *Ecce Homo* and its influence, *Explosion I* and *II*, demonstrates how Nietzsche's autobiography tells "the story of the death of the *autos* as stable subject."[14] As Kofman puts it, "*Ecce Homo* est l'autobiographie la plus 'depersonnalisée' qui soit."[15] McDonald concludes: "It spells the death of the *bios* as well if the life of the living finds its source in two parents to whom one is attached by blood."[16] Instead, to overcome this built-in death of life-writing, of all writing, one must risk madness by a form of self-creation to the point of self-apotheosis, giving birth to oneself as a being who is sui generis. Of course, to pursue this quest would mean one becomes a child of Nietzsche's self-romance in *Ecce Homo,* ever ready to strike out in defense of one's "Göttlichkeit."

Another approach to this modern problem of the vanished mediator of the patriarchal tradition, according to Lacan's late work, is to do what he claims Joyce does in his work, invent *le sinthome,* an individual makeshift linguistic suture of one's own to supplement, support, and keep attached to each other the psyche's conflicting parts. Turning the symptom of one's ever-incipient borderline psychosis—the modern subject's defining situation—into *le sinthome* means for Joyce that he receives all of his *jouissance* out of the materiality of the words he creates, especially those in *Finnegans Wake.* As Henry Kripps sensibly concludes in *Fetish: An Erotics of Culture,*

Lacan appears to be recommending that we invent our own fetishes, but never forget they are such. We would all become then like a self-conscious Queequeg, the South Pacific islander in *Moby-Dick,* making an idol to contain and give shape to our otherwise downward spiral into psychic chaos. When Nietzsche refers, reverentially and ironically, to Zarathustra in *Ecce Homo,* both the character and the book, it certainly seems like he is doing just this. But is this therapeutic expedient enough to guard against the seductions of madness that would make one a god, or at least a god's favorite, "a disciple of the god Dionysus," something Nietzsche also repeatedly claims here and throughout his last works and letters?[17]

Badiou's theory of the truth-event and truth-procedures may provide a useful, somewhat different approach to the problem of having two "natures" that are impossible to reconcile or live with. Recall that Badiou claims that mathematics and Being are the same, that Being, like mathematics, is composed of infinite multiples, without end or inherent order. Any order can then be axiomatically determined and defined by human agency, as in the construction of sets in set theory. The psychic situation of a split self or two natures in one breast, as Goethe famously called it, would then be one in which the being of one axiomatic order would be founded on the void of another, always already potentially emerging new axiomatic order.

What this means for *Ecce Homo* is that as its readers we have to do exactly the opposite of what Sarah Kofman recommends; that is, we should not try to avoid contamination by Nietzsche's emergently psychotic text, his two natures, but instead, insofar as we are his readers, we should testify to his and its truth-event, that the split in the text between two visions of natural order, inorganic and organic, is just the tip of the infinite iceberg of possible visions of order, something that Nietzsche clearly recognizes in *Ecce Homo* and throughout his later work, especially. By our creative or active reading, what we do as *his children of the event of the death of God* is interpret this text and all his works accordingly, that is, as the logic of the event requires: "In diesem Augenblick, wo ich dies schreibe, bringt die Post mit einen Dionysos-Kopf."[18] In my translation, "In this instant, as I write this, the mail brings me a Dionysus-head." How well, how actively, how creatively we can read *Ecce Homo*, Nietzsche's corpus as a whole, and indeed our own modernity, is finally determined, I think, by how effectively we can accommodate such wild textual elements as this.

6

Nietzsche's Critical Vortex: On the Global Tragedy of Theoretical Man

Marc Redfield, in his introduction to *Legacies of Paul de Man*, recalls from the years of the Ford and Carter administrations the "acrid debates about deconstruction and the 'Yale School' and the bitter, high-profile purgings of junior faculty ranks at places like Yale and Princeton" as part of what we associate with our image of Paul de Man, who more than "twenty years after his death" still "remains a haunting presence in the American academy."[1] Redfield goes on to claim that even today, "deserving scholars still sometimes suffer for being closely linked to de Manian theory."[2] He notes that while many, perhaps most, critics now are content to say "theory is dead," even if they then do (or claim to do) theory themselves in some sense of their own, they decry de Man's brand of theory, if it comes up, often reacting to it as if to the specter of all they dread most: "De Man stands for a 'theory' that again and again must be discovered to have died of natural causes, a victim of time, history, and it own internal inadequacies," and like "the literal body of the theorist, it was once alive; now it is not; it should have the decency to rest quietly in its tomb."[3] Of course, the discovery, four years after his death in 1987, of de Man's infamous wartime journalism, in which he clearly collaborated with the anti-Semitic agenda of the Nazis' occupation of his native Belgium, has something to do with this reaction, but more apparently in the sense of giving an excuse, a powerful progressive-sounding rationale, for those who hate de Man's influence, in order to keep attempting to bury it once and for all, once again.

I bring up this complex of reactions to de Man—by the many unnamed critics and by Redfield—because I think that it reflects in miniature the critical reaction to what Nietzsche, in his new preface "Attempt at Self-Criticism" that he adds to the 1886 edition of *The Birth of Tragedy,* states is the primary task of his first book, often obscured by his fustian rhetoric, namely: "*to look at science through the prism of the artist, but also to look at art through the prism of life,*" "*die Wissenschaft unter der Optik des Künstlers zu sehn, die Kunst aber unter der des Lebens.*"[4] "Prism" is a bit too specific, I think, since *der Optik* means what we generally mean by "optics," the science of seeing, perhaps, if we remember Newton, a premier gateway to modern physics.

Nietzsche, in any event, strongly intends this constantly circulating irony. By such irony, as well as by the seeming meaning of statements that carry it, Nietzsche, like de Man with his own ironies, is challenging the right of science—the way we moderns generally do knowledge—even to exist, and certainly to exist in any kind of innocent business-as-usual mindset, that is, to exist without the self-conscious burden of a profoundly bad conscience about what it does. I have addressed this dimension of de Man's haunting presence in the profession, the status of his theory as its bad conscience, in *Empire Burlesque: The Fate of Critical Theory in Global America.*[5] Now I want to address Nietzsche's tragic critique of science in his first book, and its upshot in one of his last, *The Anti-Christ.*

First, however, I need to recall the basic argument of *The Birth of Tragedy.* To do so, I will invoke its most famous "optical" conceit from the opening of section 9:

Everything that rises to the surface in dialogue,

the Apolline part of Greek tragedy, appears simple, transparent, beautiful. In this sense the dialogue is a copy of the Hellene, whose nature is expressed in dance, because in dance the greatest strength is still only potential, although it is betrayed by the suppleness and luxuriance of movement. Thus the language of Sophocles' heroes surprises us by its Apolline definiteness and clarity, so that we feel as if we are looking straight into the innermost ground of its being, and are somewhat astonished that the road to this ground is so short. But if we once divert our gaze from the character of the hero as it rises to the surface and becomes visible—fundamentally, it is no more than an image of light [*Lichtbild*] projected on to a dark wall, i.e. appearance [*Erscheinung*] through and through—if, rather, we penetrate to the myth which projects itself in these bright reflections, we suddenly experience a phenomenon which inverts a familiar optical one. When we turn away blinded after a strenuous attempt to look directly at the sun, we have dark coloured patches before our eyes, as if their purpose were to heal them; conversely, those appearances of the Sophoclean hero in images of light, in other words, the Apolline quality of the mask, are the necessary result of gazing into the inner, terrible depths of nature—radiant patches as it were, to heal a gaze seared by gruesome night. Only in this sense may we believe that we have grasped the serious and significant concept of "Greek serenity" [*Heiterkeit*] correctly; admittedly, wherever one looks at present one comes

across a misunderstood notion of this as "cheer-
fulness," something identified with a condition
of unendangered ease and comfort.[6]

Here is the core of the conceit in the original:

> Wenn wir bei einem kräftigen Versuch, die
> Sonne ins Auge zu fassen, uns geblendet abwen-
> den, so haben wir dunkle farbige Flecken gleich-
> sam als Heilmittel vor den Augen; umgekehrt
> sind jene Lichtbilderscheinungen des sophok-
> leischen Helden, kurz das Apollinische der
> Maske, notwendige Erzeugungen eines Blickes
> ins Innere und Schreckliche der Natur, gleich-
> sam leuchtende Flecken zur Heilung des von
> grausiger Nacht versehrten Blickes.[7]

Just as *Wissenschaft* means all of the sciences—natural, social, and
human—or the way we moderns produce knowledge, and not just
the natural sciences; so too *Versuch* means "attempt," "try," "trial,"
or "experiment"—the meaning that would seem best here, the one
with a playful irony that still bites.

The Dionysian principle of ecstatic rapture has at its base this
abyss of being, which is like the unknowable thing in itself behind
all appearances in Kant and Schopenhauer, except that, as in
Schopenhauer, we can know the ground of existence via the experience of our own wills, which never cease from striving, creating,
and destroying in the course of our lives, unless we are able to stand
back from them, thanks to art or asceticism, to reflect disinterest-
edly upon their therapeutic Apolline images, thereby escaping, in
these privileged moments, from the pleasures and pains of human
existence. Within each authentic tragedy, the protagonist and the
attentive audience experience such a visionary moment in which

they can intuit by tragic feeling the unknowable reality lying beyond all human knowledge:

> If the result of our analysis has been that in
> tragedy the Apolline, thanks to its deception,
> wins a complete victory over the primal,
> Dionysiac element of music, and uses the latter
> for its own purposes, in order to lend the great-
> est possible clarity to the drama, we must now
> add one very important qualification, namely
> that the Apolline deception is punctured and de-
> stroyed where it matters most of all. If drama,
> with the help of music, spreads out all its move-
> ments and figures before us with such inwardly
> illuminated clarity, as if we were seeing a tissue
> being woven on a rising and falling loom, it also
> produces, taken as a whole, an effect which goes
> *beyond all effects of Apolline art.* In the total effect
> of tragedy the Dionysiac gains the upper hand
> once more; it closes with a sound which could
> never issue from the realm of Apolline art.
> Thereby Apolline deception is revealed for what
> it is: a persistent veiling, for the duration of the
> tragedy, of the true Dionysiac effect, an effect so
> powerful, however, that it finally drives the
> Apolline drama itself into a sphere where it be-
> gins to speak with Dionysiac wisdom and where
> it negates itself and its Apolline visibility. *Thus*
> *the difficult relationship of the Apolline and the*
> *Dionysiac in tragedy truly could be symbolized by a*
> *bond of brotherhood between the two deities.*
> *Dionysos speaks the language of Apollo, but finally*
> *it is Apollo who speaks that of Dionysos. At which*

point the supreme goal of tragedy, and indeed of all art, is attained.[8]

The German of these italicized lines is:

> So wäre wirklich das schwierige Verhältnis des
> Apollinischen und des Dionysischen in der
> Tragödie durch einen Bruderbund beider Gott-
> heiten zu symbolisieren: Dionysus redet die
> Sprache des Apollo, Apollo aber schließlich die
> Sprache des Dionysus: womit das höchste Ziel des
> Tragödie und der Kunst überhaupt erreicht ist.[9]

Much can be said that has not been said about this brother-bond, just as much can be said about the scrambling of sexual identity in the family romance that gives birth to tragedy. But I will just note the following: Dionysus is figured as father, and as brother, yet Apollo, while being a brother, is said to father all of the Olympiad, and the unknowable ground of being, the Will, is said to be its womb, to be the primal mother, and yet it is Apollo and Diony-sus who procreate Attic tragedy repeatedly until Euripides and Socrates, their pale, demonic parodies, produce the undead triplets of Euripides' drama, New Attic Comedy and the belated pseudo-dithyramb of the later classical age, and those virtual bourgeois proto-novels, with Socrates as the new demonic hero, the Platonic dialogues. Be this as it may, we should not lose sight of the fact that the defensive mediation of the Apolline language of images perfects its clarity to the point of becoming transparent, like a scrim, a tis-sue, a finely woven delicate fabric, a text in short, through which we see the god but also feel the Dionysiac reverberations in the vortex of the World-Will at work—or rather, at play. Whether in honor of one god, many, or none, the tragic genre ever repeats the same self-creating and self-destroying textual logic, Nietzsche reveals in this passage. He symbolizes this logic in the figure of the Aeon, that divine, cosmic child whom Heraclitus envisions building and destroying worlds, like sand-creations, beside the waters of eternity. For Nietzsche, this mythic scene depicts perfectly the game that the primordial Will repeatedly plays with itself.[10]

This vision of tragedy as text, genre, and exemplary form of art is also, for Nietzsche, a vision of the noblest form of life, because it both recognizes the often courageous and resourceful aspirations of human beings heroically to transcend their finitude and performs the terrible and inevitable collapse of those sublime aspirations due to the earthly conditions of mortal existence. The protagonists of Greek tragedy are not to be dismissed as fools of life in a process of despairing resignation; instead, they are to be self-consciously emulated in their human, all-too-human aspirations, and in their more than human heroic acceptance of the awful cost of such memorable aspiration. Though the Greeks best realized the possibilities of tragedy in all these respects, anyone from any time can be instructed by their achievement in a tragic culture of cheerful pessimism, a pessimism from strength, not from weakness and despair, from overflowing life that wants to test itself against the hardest obstacle. Anyone can be instructed by this vision, that is, except Socrates and all his heirs, like us moderns, who believe, as he does, that the terms and conditions of human existence can be *"corrected."*[11] "Theoretical man" (*den Typus des theoretischen Menschen*), as Nietzsche calls the human type Socrates embodies, is incapable of tragic wisdom because the "logical drive which appeared in Socrates was completely incapable of turning against itself."[12] That is, until the great German philosophers, for early Nietzsche: Kant and Schopenhauer. Thanks to them, the logical drive of modernity is able to turn against itself, and move to transform science, the form of life of theoretical man par excellence, into art, into tragic art—based on the model of Wagner's music drama.

Before this can happen, however, the culture of theoretical man must complete the modern imperialistic project and take full possession of the entire planet, so that then when it turns against itself, all of humanity can be affected for the first time in history as science turns (in)to tragic art for its redemption:

> Consider for a moment how, after Socrates, the
> mystagogue of science, one school of philosophy
> follows another, like wave upon wave; how an
> unimaginable, universal greed for knowledge,
> stretching across most of the cultured world,
> and presenting itself as the true task for anyone
> of higher abilities, led science on to the high
> seas, from which it could never again be driven
> completely; and how for the first time, thanks to
> this universality, a common network of thought
> was stretched over the whole globe [*Erdball*],
> with prospects of encompassing even the laws of
> the entire solar system; when one considers all
> this, along with the astonishingly high pyramid
> of knowledge we have at present, one cannot do
> other than regard Socrates as the vortex [*Wirbel*]
> and turning-point [*Wendepunkt*] of so-called
> world history . . . At present, however, science,
> spurred on by its powerful delusion [that it can
> correct existence by reason], is hurrying unstoppably to its limits, where the optimism hidden
> in the essence of logic will founder and break
> up. For there is an infinite number of points on
> the periphery of the circle of science [like Kant's
> and Schopenhauer's critiques of the limits of science and theory], and while we have no way of
> foreseeing how the circle could ever be completed, a noble and gifted man inevitably en-

counters, before the mid-point of his existence, boundary points on the periphery like this [limit], where he stares into that which cannot be illuminated [such as the thing in itself]. When, to his horror, he sees how logic curls up around itself at these limits and finally bites its own tail, then a new form of knowledge breaks through, *tragic knowledge* [*die tragisch Erkenntnis*], which, simply to be endured, needs art for protection and medicine.[13]

Erkenntnis also means "cognition," even "perception." So it takes on more of an embodied character than our more abstract word "knowledge" does, except for its idiomatic usages in sexual contexts.

Nietzsche believes that the logic of Kant's critique of scientific reason and its optimism demonstrates the limits of that reason, because it has proven that we cannot know things in themselves but only how they must appear to us, so that what we conclude are laws of nature we can only validly hold to be laws for us and our nature. That is, what critical reflection on science and its methods and laws shows us is that we can only know how our own minds must work to perceive and understand our human world. What is the case for other beings, like animals, or other possible rational beings, depends entirely upon the structures of their apparatus of mind. As we now know, of course, the world perceived by different beings, or even registered by different instruments, is indeed a remarkably variable phenomenon. Similarly, despite Kant's confidence that we can know by self-intuition the necessary structures of our minds, so that he could rule out of court, for instance, the very possibility of any other kind of geometry than Euclid's, we know now that this is far from the case, when there are many possible geometries, which suggest not only that Kant drew a false conclusion with respect to Euclidean geometry, but also that his original intuition into the supposed universal structure of the human mind was most likely incorrect.

Nietzsche, typically, goes even further, believing that we cannot know with certainty anything but the appearances to us of whatever it is we are perceiving—their true natures are unknowable. Later in his career he draws the logical conclusion from this view, namely, that all we can know is phenomenal, and that there is no reason to assume or project an underlying essence, or thing in itself. But for now he is content to show that via Kant and, he magnanimously adds, Schopenhauer, the optimistic theoretical dialectic of Socrates, which acts as if all of existence must have a reason to it and where it does not, there it may be corrected and provided one by science, is in the modern world turning against itself precisely in the way that Socrates' logic did not in his own time. Consequently, only the art of tragedy, as Nietzsche has presented it and Wagner can perform it, can save us now, by communicating to us, so that we wholly participate in the rapture, the ecstatic ravishment, of Dionysian music reborn.

As we can see, the history of science, Socratic culture, and theoretical humanity, like that of the tragic genre itself, as well as its classical textual forms, all belong, ironically enough, to the same set, that of "things that are tragedies." Needless to say, such an overdetermined pattern would appear to verge on the disturbingly obsessive, even fetishistic. However that may be, the elements of this tragic set take the form of a romantic irony that allegorizes, as Paul de Man might say, the habitual way Nietzsche here reads such irony, via these very "texts" he writes.

Such romantic irony, as I detail in *Tragic Knowledge: Yeats's Autobiography and Hermeneutics,* posits polar opposites as general categories under which the differences in a field of experience may be organized hierarchically under them, and then puts these general categories into conflict with each other, usually unequal conflict, with one of the two categories ultimately being privileged in the contest.[14] But unlike the operation of the Hegelian dialectic, and like deconstruction, there is no definitive resolution at the end of the process, but at best only provisional ones to be followed in principle by the infinite repetition of the circle of self-conscious oppositions and their perpetually interchangeable variations and refinements. The mind's movement in the case of such romantic irony is simultaneously onward and upward, to a sublime point hovering over the field of experience so that the mind may move between this sublime summit and this abysmal field, endlessly. The previous image of the snake that eats its own tail, a traditional figure symbolizing eternity, which returns nightmarishly in the "Vision and the Riddle" chapter of *Thus Spoke Zarathustra,* can nicely exemplify how via this romantic irony Nietzsche begins to read himself in *The Birth of Tragedy.* In *Zarathustra,* of course, the snake has attached itself in a sleeping shepherd's throat, and the circle it may be said to form is truly a vicious one. Zarathustra responds to this visionary scene by shouting to the young shepherd, who we learn later is an earlier version of himself, "bite, bite!" This violent gesture of biting the snake's head off and spitting it forth now symbolizes the eternal recurrence of the same. The same image returns, with a significant difference, so that we cannot say that Nietzsche simply maintains this form of romantic irony without revision from the beginning to the end of his career.

But what are we to make of Nietzsche's allegory of reading in *The Birth of Tragedy?* I think we must conclude that this work performs itself as an example of what it celebrates, making early Nietzsche embody the trope of tragic irony. That is, this text enacts the movement from science to art that it calls for, which is why when it is read as anything other than what it is—that is, when it is read primarily as critical philosophy, as cultural history, as aesthetic theory, it is found wanting. While critics have speculated that *The Birth of Tragedy* may indeed be such a self-reflexive work, as in Paul de Man's famous essay "Genesis and Genealogy," they do not agree, as in Henry Staten's equally famous critique of de Man in his *Nietz-sche's Voice,* on what kind of tragedy it becomes in the course of its unfolding: Sophoclean, Euripidean, bourgeois *Trauerspiel,* Wagnerian music drama, and so on.[15] I am satisfied to make the point that it is a tragedy of the sort that it recognizes as such: the metahistorical and global drama of modern theoretical man.

Assuming that this is so, what would be so bad, really, if theoretical man's culture would take over the world as it appears to be finally doing now, giving each human being reason to believe optimistically that science, in the largest sense, could ultimately correct existence as a whole and every aspect of it? For an admittedly speculative response to this question, I offer the following analysis of Nietzsche's late polemic, the first volume of his "revaluation of all values," *The Anti-Christ,* in which a closely related, but in the final analysis strikingly different trope, savagely comic catachresis, provides the basis for its allegory of reading.

In "Against Nature: On Northrop Frye and Critical Romance," the central chapter of *The Romance of Interpretation: Visionary Criticism from Pater to de Man,* I first critiqued, using *The Anti-Christ,* the nihilistic consequences of the culture of theoretical man as practiced and rationalized by Frye and his critical rivals.[16] My critique here, however, will focus on Nietzsche exclusively and go further in demonstrating the position that he is forced to adopt to mount his polemic in this text against Christianity, while being rather fair, often even magnanimous, ultimately, to Jesus in his philological analysis and insightful portrayal of the psychological type of the redeemer.

Sections 29–39 of *The Anti-Christ* define Nietzsche's Jesus as the psychological type of the redeemer in sharp opposition both to the explicit words of the New Testament (though allowing for a good philologist being able to read between the lines therein) and Renan's or any other contemporaneous expert's critical historical account. Here is Nietzsche's opening salvo from section 29:

The polar opposite of struggle, of any feeling of doing-battle, has become instinct here [in Jesus]: an incapacity for resistance has become morality here ("resist not evil," the most profound saying of the Gospels, the key to their meaning in a certain sense), blessedness in peace, in gentleness, in an *inability* to be an enemy. What are the "glad tidings"? That the true life, the eternal life has been found—it is not just a promise, it exists, it is in *each of you:* as a life of love, as love without exceptions or rejections, without distance. Everyone is a child of God—Jesus did not claim any special privileges—as a child of God, everyone is equal to everyone else . . . Our whole notion, our cultural notion of "spirit" made absolutely no sense in the world where Jesus lived. The rigorous language of physiology would use a different word here: the word "idiot." We are familiar with a condition where the *sense of touch* is pathologically over-sensitive and recoils from all contact, from grasping any solid objects. Just follow this sort of physiological *habitus* to its ultimate consequences—as an instinct of hatred for *every* reality, as a flight into the "unimaginable," into the "inconceivable," as an aversion to every formula, to every concept of space and time, to everything solid, to every custom, institution, church, as a being-at-home in a world that has broken off contact with every type of reality, a world that has become completely "internal," a "true" world, an "eternal" world . . . "The kingdom of God is *in each of you.*"[17]

Nietzsche is making Jesus sound like a real decadent, a perverse hybrid made up out of Roderick Usher from Poe's "The Fall of the House of Usher" and Prince Myshkin from Dostoevsky's *The Idiot.* The figure of speech that provides the model for his characterization (or caricature) is simple catachresis, of the sort such as "the table has a broken leg." Such catachresis is a form of metaphor but not like the usual type in which two things, with their distinctive proper meanings, are identified in one figurative sense, which they can be said imaginatively to share, as in the case of the expression "the king is a lion." Here two words, king and lion, are identified as one by the copula ("is") in another, more imaginative than literal way. With the catachresis "the table has a broken leg," there is only the figurative expression presented. We can analytically reconstruct by inference the logically prior metaphorical identification involved in this expression between the human body and its parts and the table and its parts, but this is a labored pedantic absurdity that no one has ever gone through in the normal flow of everyday life and ordinary language—except when it is interrupted by such academic exercises as this one. We know immediately what is meant by "the table has a broken leg," even though we are actually operating in the figurative realm when we say this. Jesus, as Nietzsche presents him, is similarly operating in a world made up entirely out of "broken table-legs," only even more radically, of all "broken table-legs," with their accompanying visionary crutches! Nietzsche's Jesus is thus simple catachresis that is not so simple, after all, but doubled or squared: comically, satirically perfected.

Nietzsche begins to express sympathy, even compassion, for his Jesus when he thinks how thoroughly perverted the message of the glad tidings became in the hands of the disciples, and especially Paul. Nietzsche's great bon mot, "there was really only one Christian, and he died on the cross," sums up this motif of the polemic.[18] But Nietzsche's focus on the essentially childlike and indeed childish vision of Jesus underscores his point that Jesus was a living catachresis, an embodied symbol of the ultimate utopian state of being, for Socratic or theoretical man:

> It bears repeating that I am against introducing
> [as Renan and other modern critics do] the fa-
> natic into the type of the redeemer. Renan's term
> *imperieux* nullifies the type all by itself. The "glad
> tidings" of the contradiction [between the world
> and the self] is gone; the kingdom of faith be-
> longs to the *children;* the faith expressed here is
> not a hard-won faith—it is here, it has been from
> the start, it is, as it were, an infantilism that has
> receded into spirituality. Physiologists, at least,
> are familiar with cases where delayed puberty is
> the result of an organism's degeneration.—A
> faith like this does not get angry, does not lay
> blame, does not defend itself: it does not bran-
> dish "the sword"—it does not have the slightest
> suspicion that it might ever separate things from
> each other. It does not prove itself with miracles,
> rewards, or promises, certainly not "through
> scriptures": at every moment it is its own miracle,
> its own reward, its own proof, its own "kingdom
> of God." This faith does not formulate itself ei-
> ther—it *lives,* it resists formulas. Of course, acci-
> dents of environment, language, and context
> will dictate a determinate sphere of concepts: the
> first form of Christianity dealt *only* with Jewish-
> Semitic concepts (—the eating and drinking at
> the Last Supper is one such concept, one that
> was badly misused by the church, which misused
> everything Jewish). But you should guard against
> seeing this as more than a sign language, a semi-

ology, an opportunity for allegories, an excuse for parables. For this anti-realist, speech is made possible precisely by *not* taking words literally.[19]

Nietzsche here combines his two earliest and longest continuing methods of critical reading and cultural analysis, philology and physiology, to bring home his point that Jesus was mad, but mad like the holy fool in medieval times was mad: blessed like the children.

But Nietzsche goes on, and in doing so, begins to make Jesus sound increasingly strangely attractive and uncannily familiar:

> Jesus could be called a "free spirit," using the word somewhat loosely—he does not care for solid things: the word *kills,* everything solid *kills.* The concept, the *experience* of "life" as only he knew it, repelled every type of word formula, law, faith, or dogma. He spoke only about what was inside him most deeply: "life" or "truth" or "light" are his words for the innermost—he saw everything else, the whole of reality, the whole of nature, language itself, as having value only as sign, a parable.[20]

To me, this portrait of Jesus begins to sound like an ever closer approximation to the major features of Nietzsche's own ideal self-image. Just consider the following:

> This sort of symbolism *par excellence* is positioned outside all religion, all cult concepts, all history, all natural science, all experience, all knowledge, all politics, all psychology, all books, all art—his "knowing" is just *pure stupidity* concerning the fact *that* things like this exist. He does not know anything about *culture, even in*

passing, he does not need to struggle against it—
he does not negate it.[21]

Except for the extremity, these radical disavowals (and the "pure stupidity"), this vision that Nietzsche projects onto Jesus could be a proclamation from the teacher of the eternal recurrence and *amor fati.*

Similarly, Nietzsche's Jesus eliminates completely "the concepts of guilt and punishment," as well as the concept of reward in an afterlife: there is only this life which is also eternal now in this moment. "'Sin,' any distance between God and man: these are abolished—*this is what the 'glad tidings' are all about.* Blessedness is not a promise, it has no strings attached: it is the *only* reality—everything else is just a symbol used to speak about it."[22] This blessedness sounds remarkably close to Nietzsche's innocence of becoming:

> This state [of blessedness] projects itself into a
> new *practice,* the genuinely evangelical practice.
> Christians are not characterized by their "faith":
> Christians act, they are characterized by a *different* way of acting. By the fact that they do not
> offer any resistance, in their words or in their
> heart, to people who are evil to them. By the
> fact that they do not make any distinction between foreigners and natives, between Jews and
> non-Jews . . . By the fact that they do not get
> angry at anyone or belittle anyone . . . All of this
> is fundamentally a single proposition, all of this
> is the result of a single instinct.—The life of the
> redeemer was nothing other than *this* practice—
> even his death was nothing else.[23]

The exalted states that Nietzsche celebrates throughout his career—from tragic knowledge to the sublime feeling of the gay science to superhuman laughter to the innocence of becoming—may all be intimately related to this blessedness, perhaps as positive forms to their de-differentiation, or as primary text to parodic gloss, but the ironic spectral play of polemic appears to be moving toward a recognition scene:

> He no longer needed formulas, rites for interact-
> ing with God—or even prayer. He settled his ac-
> counts with the whole Jewish doctrine of
> atonement and reconciliation; he knew how the
> *practice* of life is the only thing that can make
> you feel "divine," "blessed," "evangelic," like a
> "child of God" at all times. "Atonement" and
> "praying for forgiveness" are *not* the way to God:
> *only the evangelical practice* leads to God, in fact
> it *is* "God."—What the evangel *did away with*
> was the Judaism of the concepts of "sin," "for-
> giveness of sin," "faith," "redemption through
> faith"—the whole Jewish *church doctrine* was re-
> jected in the "glad tidings."[24]

This is because, as Nietzsche concludes this penultimate section on the psychological type of the redeemer, the "profound instinct for how we must *live* to feel as if we are 'in heaven,' to feel as if we are 'eternal,' given that we do not feel *remotely* as if we are in heaven when we behave in any other way: this, and this alone, is the psychological reality of 'redemption.'—A new way of life, *not* a new faith."[25] Nietzsche strikes here at both Catholic and Protestant versions of faith, since the Christian, really to imitate Christ, must practice this new way of life not for reward in the afterlife, according to the sanctions of the priests, nor simply parade faith alone (as opposed to faith and works), as the sole justification for such salvation; no, the good Christian, like Nietzsche's Jesus, must radically be and live differently, having metabolized, embodied, and made instinct, drive, all that was precept, text, and imperative. The ultimate revisionary act is thus literally to become what one beholds—in this case, to become the living catachrestical exemplum of and ironic commentary upon the entire tradition in which one has been raised, thereby becoming truly what one is, whatever monstrous hybrid that may be—just as Nietzsche does, at the end of his career in January 1889, precisely by going mad on the streets of Turin as he throws his arms protectively around an old cart-horse whose driver is beating him.

The redeemer is the perfection of theoretical man because theoretical man, as Socrates demonstrates, seeks happiness by believing existence could be different and acting to make it so, by the irrational application of reason to all things; but blessedness, in the case of Jesus, is such happiness on steroids, the dialectical sublimation (*aufgehaben*) of such theoretical optimism—simply by being so. Modern man, like the decadent he is, is for Nietzsche one short step from the apocalyptic infantilism of the redeemer, as Nietzsche wells knows.

The final summation of his portrait of Jesus, in this context, is a sheer tour de force of hermeneutic choreography:

> If I understand anything about this great symbolist, it is that he accepted only *inner* realities as realities, as "truths"—that he considered everything else, everything natural, temporal, spatial, historical, to be just a sign, an excuse for parable. The concept "son of man" is not some concrete person belonging to history, someone individual or unique, but rather an "eternal" facticity, a psychological symbol that has been redeemed from the concept of time. The same hold true again and in the highest sense for the *God* of this typi-

cal symbolist, for the "kingdom of God," for the
"kingdom of heaven," and for the filial relation
to God. Nothing is less Christian than the *ecclesi-
astical crudity* of God as a *person,* of a "kingdom
of God" that is *yet to come,* a "kingdom of heaven"
in the *beyond,* a "son of God" as the *second person*
in the Trinity. This is all (if you will excuse the
expression) one big *fist* in the eye (what an eye it
is!) of the evangel; a *world-historical cynicism* in
the derision of symbols . . .[26]

Suddenly, out of the space of the ellipsis, comes an abysmal parable in the clarifying guise of a casual interpretation:

But it is obvious—although probably not to
everyone—what the signs "father" and "son"
suggest: the word "son" expresses the *entrance*
into a feeling of the total transfiguration of all
things (blessedness), and the word "father" expresses *this feeling itself,* the feeling of eternity, of
perfection . . . The "kingdom of God" is not
something you wait for; it does not have a yes-
terday or a day after tomorrow; it will not arrive
in a "thousand years"—it is an experience of the
heart; it is everywhere and it is nowhere.[27]

Here is the German original of this passage:

Aber es liegt ja auf der Hand, was mit den
Zeichen "Vater" und "Sohn" angerührt wird—
nicht auf jeder Hand, ich gebe es zu: mit dem
Wort "Sohn" ist der Eintritt in das Gesammt-
Ver-klärungs-Gefühl aller Dinger (die Seligheit)

ausgedrückt, mit dem Word "Vater" dieses Gefühl
selbst, das Ewigkeits-, das Vollendungs-Gefühl.[28]

The only slightly distorted echoes of Nietzsche's most famous formulations and slogans here suggest that Nietzsche, in giving this
extraordinary reading, is beginning to recognize, through the increasingly transparent mask of his redeemer type, the transfiguring
outlines of his own radiant features. And since *der Eintritt* does mean
"entrance," but more in the sense of bodily opening or the opening
of a mechanical device, we may want to envision the virtually psychotic Nietzsche in this passage, coming tragically into the Father
yet only through the divine comedy of the Son, smiling in his self-
critical vortex, but whether ultimately in darkening panic or in
dawning joy, is naturally enough anybody's guess.

The world-historical cynicism of Paul's and the early church's
perversion of Jesus, making him into a compendium of the saviors
of the mystery religions, now becomes a "world-historical irony"
that borders no longer on savage satire but on savage tragedy:

> Anyone looking for signs that an ironic divinity
> is keeping his finger in the great game of the
> world will find them in the *enormous question
> mark* called Christianity. The fact that humanity
> knelt down before the opposite of the origin, the
> meaning, the *right* of the evangel, the fact that
> in the concept of "church," humanity canonized
> the very thing the "bearer of glad tidings" felt to
> be *beneath* him, *behind* him—you will not find a
> greater example of *world-historical irony.*[29]

I may not be able to suggest what Nietzsche really means by his reading of "son of man" or "father" and "son" given above; but I can suggest that in this final formulation he identifies with Jesus in his

world-historical situation, even as the Epicurean, cosmic ironist here resembles, more than passingly, the Heraclitean Aeon, the divine child of the tragedy of existence, to which in *The Birth of Tragedy,* that most questionable of first books, as we have seen, Nietzsche originally introduces his readers. With his even more questionable, virtually occult intuition here in *The Anti-Christ* into the father-son dynamics of the Trinity—given so blithely as if it were all obvious—Nietzsche performs a metaleptic turn, a transumptive catachresis, upon the catachrestical troping that Jesus performs upon his world, every bit as powerful as any humanly imaginable. In short, Nietzsche tops Jesus and his Father, indeed the total set of that or any world. This conclusion, like that of Jesus, bodes ill, to say the least, for our global modernity.

Nietzsche's critical vortex is this ironic, self-destroying sign of the allegory of reading into the life of tropes he performs repeatedly as the singular ethical practice of truth as event for modern theoretical man. Given such a denouement, there can be little wonder that so many people, so very often, continue to wish the impossible—that he, Paul de Man, and theory really could be dead: once and for all . . .

NOTES

Chapter 1

1. Sarah Juliet Laura and Karen Embry, "A Zombie Manifesto: The Nonhuman Condition in the Era of Advanced Capitalism," *boundary 2* 35, no. 1 (Spring 2008): 91.

2. Friedrich Nietzsche, *Daybreak: Thoughts on the Prejudices of Morality,* ed. Maudemarie Clark and Brian Leiter, trans. R. J. Hollingdale (Cambridge, Eng., and New York: Cambridge University Press, 1997), 5.

3. James I. Porter, *Nietzsche and the Philology of the Future* (Stanford, Calif.: Stanford University Press, 2000).

4. F. A. Lange, *The History of Materialism and Criticism of Its Present Importance in Three Volumes,* trans. E. C. Trench, intro. Bertrand Russell (London: Routledge, 1925, 2000, 2001; orig. German ed. 1865, rev. 2nd ed. 1873). This text is based on the second edition.

5. Nietzsche, *Daybreak,* 65. For the reader's convenience, throughout this book, I refer to specific passages in Nietzsche's works by "aphorism" or section number in the text, and by page number in the notes.

6. Ibid., 71–72.

7. Ibid., 68.

8. Ibid., 69.

9. Ibid., 78.

10. Ibid., 74.

11. Ibid.

12. Ibid., 74–75.

13. Ibid., 76.

14. Ibid.

Chapter 2

1. In saying this I do mean to describe an editorial convention being used, rather than how any editor may feel or write elsewhere about Nietzsche's work. Admittedly, too, none of the other editors is as naively or determinedly damning with faint praise as those I focus on in my argument here. And I have consulted all ten volumes in the series of Cambridge Texts in the History of Philosophy devoted to Nietzsche.

2. Friedrich Nietzsche, *Beyond Good and Evil,* ed. Rolf-Peter Horstmann and Judith Norman, trans. Judith Norman (Cambridge, Eng., and New York: Cambridge University Press, 2002), viii.

3. Ibid.

4. Friedrich Nietzsche, *The Gay Science,* ed. Bernard Williams, trans. Josefine Nauckhoff, poems trans. Andrea Del Caro (Cambridge, Eng., and New York: Cambridge University Press, 2001), xi–xii.

5. Friedrich Nietzsche, *Daybreak: Thoughts on the Prejudices of Morality,* ed. Maudemarie Clark and Brian Leiter, trans. R. J. Hollingdale (Cambridge, Eng., and New York: Cambridge University Press, 1997), xiii.

6. Nietzsche, *Beyond Good and Evil,* 32.

7. Nietzsche, *Daybreak,* 116.

8. Ibid., 119.

9. Ibid., 109.

10. Friedrich Nietzsche, *The Birth of Tragedy and Other Writings,* ed. Raymond Geuss and Ronald Speirs, trans. Ronald Speirs (Cambridge, Eng., and New York: Cambridge University Press, 1999), 144.

11. Nietzsche, *The Gay Science,* 373.

12. Ibid., 375–78.

13. Friedrich Nietzsche, *Selected Letters of Friedrich Nietzsche,* ed. and trans. Christopher Middleton (Indianapolis, Ind., and Cambridge, Mass.: Hackett, 1996), 206.

14. Ibid., 232–35.

Chapter 3

1. James I. Porter, *Nietzsche and the Philology of the Future* (Stanford, Calif.: Stanford University Press, 2000), 32.

2. Sarah Kofman, *Nietzsche and Metaphor,* trans. Duncan Large (Stanford, Calif.: Stanford University Press, 1993), 1.

3. Bernd Magnus, introduction to *The Cambridge Companion to Nietzsche,* ed. Bernd Magnus and Kathleen Higgins (Cambridge, Eng., and New York: Cambridge University Press, 1994), 7.

4. Friedrich Nietzsche, "On Truth and Lying in a Non-Moral Sense," in *The Birth of Tragedy and Other Writings,* ed. Raymond Geuss and Ronald Speirs, trans. Ronald Speirs (Cambridge, Eng., and New York: Cambridge University Press, 1999), 144.

5. Friedrich Nietzsche, *The Gay Science,* ed. Bernard Williams, trans. Josefine Nauckhoff, poems trans. Andrea Del Caro (Cambridge, Eng., and New York: Cambridge University Press, 2001), 193.

6. Babette E. Babich, "A Note on Nietzsche's *Chaos sive natura,*" *New Nietzsche Studies* 5, no. 3/4 and 6, no. 1/2 (Winter 2003/Spring 2004): 53–54.

7. Nietzsche, *The Gay Science,* 120.

8. Ibid., 106.

9. Jill Marsden, "Nietzsche and the Art of the Aphorism," in *A Companion to Nietzsche,* ed. Keith Ansell-Pearson (Malden, Mass.: Blackwell, 2006), 29.

10. Kathleen Marie Higgins, *Comic Relief: Nietzsche's "Gay Science"* (New York: Oxford University Press, 2000).

11. Nietzsche, *The Gay Science,* 185.

12. Ibid.

13. Ibid., 186.

14. Ibid.

15. Ibid.

16. Ibid., 162.

17. Ibid., 162–64.

18. Ibid., 158.

19. Ibid.

20. David B. Allison, *Reading the New Nietzsche: The Birth of Tragedy, The Gay Science, Thus Spoke Zarathustra, On the Genealogy of Morals* (New York: Rowman and Littlefield, 2001), 234.

21. Daniel T. O'Hara, *The Romance of Interpretation: Visionary Criticism from Pater to de Man* (New York: Columbia University Press, 1985); Jean-Pierre Mileur, *The Critical Romance: The Critic as Reader, Writer, Hero* (Madison: University of Wisconsin Press, 1990).

22. Nietzsche, *The Gay Science*, 193.

23. Ibid., 193–94.

24. Ibid., 157.

25. Ibid., 93.

26. Ibid., 190–91.

27. Ibid., 195.

28. Ibid., 192–93, section 338, "The Will to Suffer and Those Who Feel Compassion."

Chapter 4

1. Friedrich Nietzsche, *Also sprach Zarathustra*, vol. 4 of *Sämtliche Werke: Kritische Studienausgabe*, 2nd ed., ed. Giorgio Colli and Mazzino Montinari, 15 vols. (Berlin and New York: De Gruyter, 1988).

2. Friedrich Nietzsche, *Thus Spoke Zarathustra*, trans. Walter Kaufmann (New York and London: Penguin, 1954, 1966); and Friedrich Nietzsche, *Thus Spoke Zarathustra*, trans. R. J. Hollingdale (New York and London: Penguin, 1969, 2003).

3. Friedrich Nietzsche, *Thus Spake Zarathustra*, trans. Thomas Common, intro. Nicholas Davey (London: Wordsworth Classics, 1997); Friedrich Nietzsche, *Thus Spoke Zarathustra*, trans. Clancy Martin, intro. Kathleen M. Higgins and Robert C. Solomon (New York: Barnes and Noble Classics, 2005); Friedrich Nietzsche, *Thus Spoke Zarathustra*, trans. Graham Parkes (Oxford: Oxford World's Classics, 2005); and Friedrich Nietzsche, *Thus Spoke Zarathustra*, trans. Adrian Del Caro, ed. Adrian Del Caro and Robert Pippin (Cambridge, Eng.: Cambridge University Press, 2006).

4. Nietzsche, Cambridge *Zarathustra*, 58.

5. Nietzsche, Verlag de Gruyter *Zarathustra*, 100.

6. Nietzsche, Cambridge *Zarathustra*, 56.

7. Martin Heidegger, *Nietzsche: Volumes One and Two*, trans. and ed. David Farrell Krell (New York: Harper Collins, 1979, 1991).

8. David B. Allison, *Reading the New Nietzsche: The Birth of Tragedy, The Gay Science, Thus Spoke Zarathustra, On the Genealogy of Morals* (New York: Rowman and Littlefield, 2001).

9. Laurence Lampert, *Nietzsche's Teaching: An Interpretation of "Thus Spoke Zarathustra"* (New Haven, Conn.: Yale University Press, 1986); Stanley Rosen, *The Mask of Enlightenment: Nietzsche's Zarathustra*, 2nd ed., originally in Modern European Philosophy Series by Cambridge University Press (New Haven, Conn.: Yale University Press, 2004); and T. K. Seung, *Nietzsche's Epic of the Soul: Thus Spoke Zarathustra* (New York: Lexington Books, Rowman and Littlefield, 2005).

10. Nietzsche, Cambridge *Zarathustra*, 109.

11. Ibid., 108; and Nietzsche, Verlag de Gruyter *Zarathustra*, 178.

12. Nietzsche, Cambridge *Zarathustra*, 110.

13. Ibid.

14. Ibid; and Nietzsche, Verlag de Gruyter *Zarathustra*, 179.

15. Nietzsche, Cambridge *Zarathustra*, 110.

16. Ibid., 111.

17. Ibid., 112.

18. Ibid., 124; and Nietzsche, Verlag de Gruyter *Zarathustra*, 199.

19. Nietzsche, Cambridge *Zarathustra*, 125.

20. Ibid., 126; and Nietzsche, Verlag de Gruyter *Zarathustra*, 200.

21. Nietzsche, Cambridge *Zarathustra*, 126.

22. Nietzsche, Hollingdale *Zarathustra*, 341.

23. David Farrell Krell, "Consultations with the Paternal Shadow: Gasché, Derrida, and Klossowski on *Ecce Homo*," in *Exceedingly Nietzsche: Aspects of Contemporary Nietzsche Interpretation*, ed. David Farrell Krell and David Wood (London and New York: Routledge, 1988).

24. Nietzsche, Cambridge *Zarathustra*, 126.

25. Nietzsche, Verlag de Gruyter *Zarathustra*, 201–2.

26. Nietzsche, Cambridge *Zarathustra*, 127.

27. Nietzsche, Verlag de Gruyter *Zarathustra,* 202.

28. Sarah Kofman, *Explosion II: Les Enfants de Nietzsche* (Paris: Éditions Galilee, 1993).

29. Nietzsche, Cambridge *Zarathustra,* 125; and Nietzsche, Verlag de Gruyter *Zarathustra,* 200.

30. Ned Lukacher, *Time-Fetishes: The Secret History of Eternal Recurrence* (Durham, N.C.: Duke University Press, 1998); Nietzsche, Cambridge *Zarathustra,* 175; and Nietzsche, Verlag de Gruyter *Zarathustra,* 273.

31. Nietzsche, Cambridge *Zarathustra,* 176.

32. Ibid., 177; and Nietzsche, Verlag de Gruyter *Zarathustra,* 275.

33. Nietzsche, Cambridge *Zarathustra,* 174.

34. Ibid., 178.

35. Ibid., 174.

36. Ibid., 266; and Nietzsche, Verlag de Gruyter *Zarathustra,* 408.

37. Ibid.

38. Ibid.; and Nietzsche, Cambridge *Zarathustra,* 266.

Chapter 5

1. This chapter focuses on Friedrich Nietzsche, *Ecce Homo: How to Become What You Are,* trans. Duncan Large (Oxford and New York: Oxford University Press, 2007). This is the seventh English translation. Other editions and translations include *Ecce Homo: Wie Man Wird, Was Man Ist,* a Dover Thrift–like edition based on the Colli and Montinari text cited herein (Middlesex, Texas: 2006); *Ecce Homo (Nietzsche's Autobiography),* trans. Anthony M. Ludovici, in *The Complete Works of Friedrich Nietzsche,* ed. Oscar Levy, 18 vols. (Edinburgh, London, and New York: Foulis, 1909–11; vol. 17, 1911); *Ecce Homo,* trans. Clifton P. Fadiman (New York: Modern Library, 1927); *On the Genealogy of Morals and Ecce Homo,* trans. Walter Kaufmann (New York: Vintage, 1967); *Ecce Homo,* trans. R. J. Hollingdale (Hammondsworth and New York: Penguin, 1979; 2nd ed. 1992); *Ecce Homo,* trans. Thomas Wayne (New York: Algora, 2004); and *Ecce Homo,* trans. Judith Norman (Cambridge, Eng., and New York: Cambridge University Press, 2005).

2. Nietzsche, Oxford *Ecce Homo,* 7.

3. Ibid., 33.

4. Friedrich Nietzsche, *Ecce Homo,* vol. 3 of *Sämtliche Werke: Kritische Studienausgabe,* 2nd ed., ed. Giorgio Colli and Mazzino Montinari, 15 vols. (Berlin and New York: De Gruyter, 1988), 28.

5. Nietzsche, Oxford *Ecce Homo,* 31–32.

6. Ibid., 32.

7. Ibid.

8. Nietzsche, Gruyter *Ecce Homo,* 27.

9. Nietzsche, Oxford *Ecce Homo,* 68–69.

10. Nietzsche, Gruyter *Ecce Homo,* 53.

11. Nietzsche, Oxford *Ecce Homo,* 70.

12. Lawrence M. Krause and Robert J. Scherrer, "The End of Cosmology?" *Scientific American* 298, no. 3: 46–53.

13. Nietzsche, Oxford *Ecce Homo,* 10.

14. Christie McDonald, "Sarah Kofman: Effecting Self Translation," *Erudit Revue* 11, no. 2 (1998): 185.

15. Ibid.; and Sarah Kofman, *Explosion I: De l'Ecce Homo de Nietzsche* (Paris: Galilee, 1992), 29.

16. McDonald, "Kofman," 186.

17. Nietzsche, Oxford *Ecce Homo,* 10.

18. Nietzsche, Gruyter *Ecce Homo,* 11.

Chapter 6

1. Marc Redfield, ed., *Legacies of Paul de Man* (New York: Fordham University Press, 2007), 1.

2. Ibid., 2.

3. Ibid.

4. Friedrich Nietzsche, *The Birth of Tragedy and Other Writings,* ed. Raymond Geuss and Ronald Speirs, trans. Ronald Speirs (Cambridge, Eng., and New York: Cambridge University Press, 1999), 5; and Friedrich Nietzsche, *Die Geburt der Tragödie aus dem Geiste der Musik* (Frankfurt am Main and Leipzig: Insel Verlag, 1987, 2000), 12.

5. Daniel T. O'Hara, *Empire Burlesque: The Fate of Critical Culture in Global America* (Durham, N.C.: Duke University Press, 2003).

6. Nietzsche, *Birth of Tragedy,* 46–47.

7. Nietzsche, *Die Geburt der Tragödie,* 74–75.

8. Nietzsche, *Birth of Tragedy,* 103–4.

9. Nietzsche, *Die Geburt der Tragödie,* 164–65.

10. Nietzsche, *Birth of Tragedy,* 113.

11. Ibid., 66.

12. Nietzsche, *Die Geburt der Tragödie,* 114; and Nietzsche, *Birth of Tragedy,* 67.

13. Nietzsche, *Birth of Tragedy,* 74–75.

14. Daniel T. O'Hara, *Tragic Knowledge: Yeats's Autobiography and Hermeneutics* (New York: Columbia University Press, 1981).

15. Paul de Man, *Allegories of Reading: Figural Language in Rousseau, Nietzsche, Rilke, and Proust* (New Haven, Conn., and London: Yale University Press, 1979); and Henry Staten, *Nietzsche's Voice* (Ithaca, N.Y.: Cornell University Press, 1993).

16. Daniel T. O'Hara, *The Romance of Interpretation: Visionary Criticism from Pater to de Man* (New York: Columbia University Press, 1985).

17. Friedrich Nietzsche, *The Anti-Christ, Ecce Homo, Twilight of the Idols, and Other Writings,* ed. Aaron Ridley and Judith Norman, trans. Judith Norman (Cambridge, Eng., and New York: Cambridge University Press, 2005).

18. Ibid., 39.

19. Ibid., 29.

20. Ibid., 29–30.

21. Ibid.

22. Ibid.

23. Ibid., 30–31.

24. Ibid., 31.

25. Ibid.

26. Ibid.

27. Ibid., 31–32.

28. Friedrich Nietzsche, *Der Fall Wagner, Götzen-Dämmerung, Der Antichrist, Ecce Homo, Dionysus-Dithyramben, Nietzsche contra Wagner,* vol. 15 of *Sämtliche Werke: Kritische Studienausgabe,* ed. Giorgio Colli and Mazzino Montinari, 15 vols. (Berlin and New York: De Gruyter, 1967–77; 1988; 1999; 2008), 206–7.

29. Nietzsche, *The Anti-Christ,* 33.

INDEX

Absolute knowledge, 11
Adam, body of, 65
Aeon figure, 91, 106
Alien movies, 78
Allison, David, 55; *Reading the New Nietzsche,* 43
Andromeda galaxy, 81
Ansell-Pearson, Keith, 24
anti-Semitism, 85
aphorisms, Nietzsche's, 36–37
Apollo: Apolline images, 87–90; and Dionysus, 78, 89–90
ascetic, the, 10, 11–12
Athena, 78
Attic tragedy, New Attic Comedy, 78, 90. *See also* tragedy

Babich, Babette E.: "A Note on Nietzsche's *Chaos sive natura,*" 33–34
Badiou, Alain, 15, 27–28, 33–34, 66–68, 83
barbarian, the, 10
Barnes and Noble Classics, 51
Bataille, Georges, 55
"beautiful moments," 31–32, 33
Being, 23; God as center of, 69; and mathematics, 67, 83; unknowable ground of, 90; utopian state of, 99

Big Bang theory, 31, 81
birth imagery, 77–78
black hole, 28, 54, 81
Blake, William, 53; "The Female Will," 44
blessedness, 101–2, 103
Bloom, Harold, 34, 44
body's skin as metaphor, 21
boundary 2: an international journal of literature, 3, 73
Brahmins, the, 11
Buchner, Ludwig, 20
Buddha, death of, 56
Byron, George Gordon, Lord, 12

Calvin, John, 12
Cambridge Companion to Nietzsche, The: Magnus's introduction to, 30
Cambridge Texts in the History of Philosophy series, 17, 51, 73
Carter, Jimmy, 85
catachresis: upon catachresis, 30, 78; as form of metaphor, 98; Jesus as, 99
chaos, 54, 67; and Old Night principle, 34; the opposite of, 77; psychic, 83
Christianity, 66, 77; as enormous

question mark, 105; imitation of Christ, 103; Nietzsche's polemic against, 96–106
Clark, Maudemarie, 17, 20–21, 24
Coleridge, Samuel Taylor, 76
Colli, Giorgio, 51
Common, Thomas, 51
consciousness, 15, 21, 75–76
cosmological constant, 81
creativity blocked, released, 44, 48
cripples, inverse, 56
criticism: art of, 5–6; contemporary, (failure of, to read texts closely) 4, (rhetorical) 5; of Nietzsche's works, see Nietzsche, Friedrich
culture of representation, 52, 53–54

Dante Alighieri, 12; *Vita Nuova,* 37
Davey, Nicholas, 51
death: allegorical vision of, 80; of God or gods, 34–37, 53, 66, 82, 84; of life-writing, 82; of Nietzsche's father, 61–62; thought of, 40–41
deconstruction, 24, 64, 74, 95; debates about, 85
Del Caro, Adrian, 51
de Man, Paul, 24, 55, 85–86, 94, 106; *Allegories of Reading: Figural Language in Rousseau, Nietzsche, Rilke, and Proust,* 6; "Genesis and Genealogy," 96
demons, 46–47; demonic hero, 90; demonic muse-figure, 44
Derrida, Jacques, 24, 55, 62
Descartes, René, 40
dialectic: Hegelian, 95; spiral of, 11; theoretical, of Socrates, 94
Dionysus, 34, 83, 84; Apollo and, 78, 89–90; vs. "The Crucified," 50; Dionysian principle of ecstatic rapture, 88

distinction, drive for, 9–10, 12
Dostoevsky, Fyodor: *The Idiot,* 98
dreams, 14–15
drives: and counter-drives, 7–8, 22–23; for distinction, 9–10, 12; focus on, 30; Hobbesian contest of, 31; philology of, 15, 16; self-betraying truth of, 14; sublimation of, 7; totality of, 12–13, 22; unconscious, contest among, 38
dwarf, Zarathustra's, 59–60, 63–64, 66

ecstatic rapture, 79, 88, 94
ego, the, 9; casuistry of egoism, 75–77
Einstein, Albert, 67, 81
Enlightenment, the, 80; post-Enlightenment culture, 52
Epicurean irony, 106
Eros, 47
eternity, symbol of, 69, 95
ethics, 52; of reading, 27; self-critical, 28
Euclidean geometry, 93–94
Euripides, 90, 96

Fall, the, 65
feminism, 19. *See also* woman
fetishes, 83
Feuerbach, Ludwig Andreas, 20
Ford, Gerald, 85
Foucault, Michel, 55, 80
French Revolution, 67
Freud, Sigmund, 7, 38, 66, 76
Frye, Northrop, 44, 96
Fuchs, Carl, Nietzsche's letter to, 27
future: humanity of the, 24–27, 28, 46–48, 50; vision of the, 40

Gasché, Rodolphe, 62
Gast, Peter, Nietzsche's letters to, 27

Gennaro, Saint, 38
German materialism, 20
German philosophy, 91
"glad tidings," 97, 98–99, 101, 105
God: Byronic vision of, 12; as center
    of Being, 69; death of, 34–37, 53,
    82, 84; evangelical practice lead-
    ing to, 102; "kingdom" and "son"
    of, 98, 99, 104–5; and man, dis-
    tance between, 101; old, services
    of, 42. See also gods
Gödel, Kurt, 28, 69
gods: death of, 53, 66; of love and
    holiness, 11. See also God
Goethe, Johann Wolfgang von, 34,
    46, 47, 83; Dichtung und
    Wahrheit, 40
Gospels, the, 97
"Greek serenity," 88
Greek tragedy. See tragedy
Greek verse, 27
Greene, Brian: The Elegant
    Universe, 52
Gumbrecht, Hans Ulrich, 24

happiness, 10, 26, 48, 79, 103
Haraway, Donna: "Cyborg Mani-
    festo," 4–5
Hegel, Georg W. F., 95; Phenomenol-
    ogy of Spirit, 11
Heidegger, Martin, 23, 24; Being and
    Time, 40; "Who is Nietzsche's
    Zarathustra?," 55
Heraclitus, 91, 106
hermeneutics, Nietzschean, 29, 55,
    103–4
Higgins, Kathleen Marie, 51; Comic
    Relief: Nietzsche's Gay Science, 38
history, sense of, 25
Hobbes, Thomas, 31
Hollingdale, R. J., 17, 51, 61–62,
    64, 69

Horstmann, Ralph Peter, 17–18
howling dog as theme, 60–62, 64
"humanity" of the future, 24–27, 28,
    46–48, 50
hunchback episode, 56, 57–58

identity: language and, 35; loss of,
    35; personal, God and, 34; psy-
    chosexual struggle for, 44; quest
    for, 38; self-nominating, 71; sym-
    bolic, of Zarathustra, 53–55; tra-
    ditional, 53
innocence of becoming, 101–2
inspiration, Nietzsche's experience of,
    78–80
intentional/unintentional, 21
irony, 53, 55, 71, 86, 102;
    Epicurean, 106; romantic, 15, 64,
    94–95; tragic, 95; "world-
    historical" (of Christianity), 105–6

Janus (Roman god), 38
Jesus Christ, Nietzsche's view of,
    96–101, 103–6; madness of, 100;
    as redeemer, 96, 102–3, 105
Jews, 101–2; Jewish-Semitic concepts,
    99–100. See also anti-Semitism
Joyce, James, 82; Finnegans Wake, 83
Jung, Carl G., 69

Kamuf, Peggy: Signatures: The Insti-
    tution of Authorship, 52
Kant, Immanuel, 17, 18, 20, 21, 88,
    91, 92–94
Kaufmann, Walter, 51, 63
Keats, John, 44
Klossowski, Pierre, 24, 62; Nietzsche
    and the Vicious Circle, 23; Such a
    Deathly Desire, 23
knowing: self-knowledge, 9, 12–13,
    22, 30; Spinoza on, 38–39; tragic
    knowledge, 93–95

Kofman, Sarah, 55, 83; *Explosion I and II,* 66, 82; *Nietzsche and Metaphor,* 29

Krause, Lawrence M.: "The End of Cosmology?," 81

Krell, David Farrell: "Consultations with the Paternal Shadow: Gasché, Derrida, and Klossowski on *Ecce Homo,*" 62

Kripps, Henry: *Fetish: An Erotics of Culture,* 83

Kristeva, Julia, 66

Kurzweil, Ray: *The Singularity Is Near,* 52

Lacan, Jacques, 27–28, 33, 35, 66, 82–83

lake metaphor, 39

Lampert, Lawrence: *Nietzsche's Teaching,* 55

Lange, Friedrich A., 20; *History of Materialism,* 7

language, 9, 30; and identity, 35

Large, Duncan, 76

Last Supper, the, 100

Leiter, Brian, 17, 20–21, 24

Levinas, Emmanuel: *Proper Names,* 52

life: personified as woman, 32, 44

Lukacher, Ned, 69

Magnus, Bernd, 29–30

Marsden, Jill: "The Art of the Aphorism," 36

Martin, Clancy, 51

martyr, the, 10

mask-play, 8

mathematics, Being and, 67, 83

McDonald, Christie: "Sarah Kofman: Effecting Self Translation," 82

Melville, Herman: *Moby-Dick,* 83

metaphorical thinking, 29

Mileur, Jean-Pierre: *The Critical Romance: The Critic as Reader, Writer, Hero,* 44

Milton, John: *Paradise Lost,* 78

modernity, 20, 21, 34; German philosophy and, 91; global, 106; problem of, 54, 71, 84

Montinari, Mazzino, 51

morality: old, 44; traditional vs. modern, 20–21

Morris, William, 33

Napoleon Bonaparte, 53

Nazis, the, 85

Nehamas, Alexander: *Nietzsche: Life as Literature,* 6

nerve stimuli, 23, 30. *See also* drives

New Testament, the, 96–107

Newton, Isaac, 86

Nietzsche, Friedrich: criticism of, 17–18, 19–20, 86, 96, (critical amnesia) 73–74; letters, 27; madness of, 62, 81–82, 103; and philology, 6–7, 15–16, 22, ("speculative") 29, 32

works: *The Anti-Christ,* 15, 16, 86, 96–106; *Beyond Good and Evil,* 16, 21, (introduction to) 17–18; *The Birth of Tragedy,* 15, 78, 95–96, 106, ("Attempt at Self-Criticism") 86; *Chaos sive natura,* 33; *Daybreak,* 7–16, (introduction to) 17, 20–23, ("Self-Mastery and Moderation and Their Ultimate Motive") 7, ("There Are Two Kinds of Deniers of Morality") 21, (translation of) 17; *Ecce Homo,* 15, 50, 53, 62, 74, 78–84, ("Why I Am So Clever") 74, 75, ("Why I Write Such Good Books") 74, 78–80; *Experience and Invention,* 12–13; *The Gay*

Science, 15, 24, 26, 31–50, (intro-
duction to) 19–20, ("The Dying
Socrates") 26, 43, 45, ("For the
New Year") 45–46, ("Get on the
Ships") 42–43, ("The Greatest
Weight") 26, ("The Heaviest
Weight") 46, ("High Spirits") 39–
40, ("The 'Humanity' of the Fu-
ture") 26–27, 47–48, ("Incipit
Tragoedia") 26, 48, ("Long Live
Physics") 43, ("The Madman")
34, ("New Battles") 36, ("One
Thing Is Needful") 43, ("Personal
Providence") 46, ("St. Januarius")
26, 33, 36–38, 42, 48, 50, ("The
Thought of Death") 40–41,
("Vita Femina") 31–32, 43–44,
("What Knowing Means") 38–39,
43, ("Will and Wave") 43, ("The
Will to Suffer") 110n28; On the
Genealogy of Morals, 16, (intro-
duction to) 24; "On Truth and
Lying in a Non-Moral Sense," 23–
24; Thus Spoke Zarathustra: A
Book for All and None, 15, 26, 43,
51–72, ("The Bestowing Virtue")
54, ("The Convalescent") 55, 69,
(Nietzsche's discussion of) 74, 77,
79–80, 83, ("On Redemption")
55–56, ("On the Vision and the
Riddle") 55, 58–59, 67–68, 95,
("The Sign") 55, 71; translations,
16, 51–52, 61, 63, 65, 73–74,
(untranslatability) 52, 66, 68, 72
Nietzsche, Joseph, 62
nihilism, 20, 23, 46, 55, 96
nobility, 21, 26

Odysseus, 43
Oedipal quests, Oedipus complex,
44, 66
O'Hara, Daniel T.: Empire Burlesque:
The Fate of Critical Theory in
Global America, 5, 86; Radical
Parody, 5; The Romance of Inter-
pretation: Visionary Criticism from
Pater to de Man, 6, 44, ("Against
Nature: On Northrop Frye and
Critical Romance") 96; Tragic
Knowledge: Yeats's Autobiography
and Hermeneutics, 73, 94; Why
Nietzsche Now?, 6, 73
Olympiad, the, 90
One or order, 67
ontology, Badiou's, 67
"optics," 86–87
Orphic mysteries, 34
Ouroboros, 69
Overbeck, Franz, Nietzsche's letter
to, 27
overman, the, 53, 57, 66
Oxford World Classics, 51

Parkes, Graham, 51
"passion," Nietzsche's, 30, 33, 36–37,
42, 48, 50
paternal metaphor, 35, 82
Paul, Apostle, 12, 99, 105
philology, 6–7, 16, 22, 24; of drives,
15, 16; Nietzsche's "speculative,"
29, 32
philosophy: analytic, 17; as domain
of truths, 67; German, and
modernity, 91
"physical style of thinking," 27, 28
Pippin, Robert, 51
Platonic dialogues, 90
Poe, Edgar Allan: "The Fall of the
House of Usher," 98
Porter, James I., 7, 30; Nietzsche and
the Philology of the Future, 29
posthumanism, 5
power: lust for, 12. See also
will-to-power

Pre-Raphaelites, 33
Princeton University, 85
proper names, 52
Provençal poets, 33
psychoanalysis, 21–22, 66
psychomachia, 39, 43

quest-romance, 33, 37, 43–44, 45, 82

reading: as act of knowing, 39; art of, as way of life, 5–6, 8–9, 13–15; creative, 50; reading of, 29
Real, Lacan's theory of, 28, 33
redemption, 57; Jesus as redeemer, 96, 102–3, 105; self-redemption, 55
Redfield, Marc: *Legacies of Paul de Man,* 85–86
Renan, Ernest, 97, 99
revenge, spirit of, 57, 58
Right, political, 19
Roman Empire, 20
romantic irony, 15, 64, 94–95
Rosen, Stanley: *The Mask of Enlightenment,* 55

Sade, Marquis de, 12
Sage, figure of the, 11
Scherrer, Robert J.: "The End of Cosmology?," 81
Schiller, Friedrich von, 76
Schopenhauer, Arthur, 20, 88, 91, 92, 94
science, 88, 91–93, 96; existence challenged, 86; of poetry ("gay science"), 33
self-enjoyment, 11
self-genesis, 34
self-knowledge. *See under* knowing
self-nominating identity, 71
self-redemption, 55
Semele, 34
set and null-set of presented

elements, 67–68
Seung, T. K.: *Nietzsche's Epic of the Soul,* 55
Shakespeare, William: *Hamlet,* 66
Shelley, Percy Bysshe, 44
shepherd as theme, 63, 64, 65, 66, 69–70, 95
singularity, 52–53, 71
snake image, 63, 64, 65, 69, 70, 95
Socrates, 45, 47, 90, 91–92, 94; Socratic man, 99, 103
solar imagery, 26, 27, 37–38, 42, 48, 87
Solomon, Robert C., 51
Sophocles, 87, 96
Spenser, Edmund: *Faerie Queene,* 44
Spinoza, Baruch, 38–39, 43
Staten, Henry: *Nietzsche's Voice,* 96
Stevens, Wallace: "Planet on the Table," 43
Stimmung, 24–26, 40
sublimation of drives, 7
suffering, god creating, 11
superhuman, the, 11, 46; superhuman type, 75
"surd element," 28, 34, 69

"theoretical man," 91–92, 94, 96, 99, 103, 106
theory, de Manian, 85
time as a circle, 59
tragedy, 96; Greek, 78, 87, 89–92; tragic irony, 95; tragic knowledge, 93–95
translations, 51–52, 61, 63, 65, 73–74; untranslatability, 52, 66, 68, 72
transubstantiation, 65–66
Trinity, the, 104, 106
truth: crooked, 59; discovery of, 27; experimental, 37; Nietzsche defines, 23–24, 30; philosophy as

domain of, 67; self-betraying, of
  drives, 14; truth-value, 29
truth-event, 50, 106; Badiou's concept of, 15, 28, 33, 66–68, 83,
  (examples of) 67

Übermenschen, 26, 28, 82
unincorporated, the, 68–69

Vico, Giovanni Battista, 12

Wagner, Richard, 33, 40, 92, 94, 96
Whitman, Walt, 37
Will, the, 90–91; creative, 54, 57;
  willing backward, 57–58;
  will-to-love, 47; will-to-power,
  26–27, 28, 37, 47, 53, (relationship with overman) 57, 66;
  will-to-truth, will-to-conquer, 31;
  World Will, 91

Williams, Bernard, 19–20, 24
woman: and feminism, 19; as femme
  fatale, 44; life personified as, 32,
  44; matriarchy, transformation to
  patriarchy from, 34
Wordsworth, William, 44
Wordsworth Classics, 51

"Yale School," 85

Zarathustra, story of, 43, 48–50,
  51–72
Zeus myth, 34, 78
"Zombie Manifesto, A," 3, 4;
  quoted, 4–5

ABOUT THE AUTHOR

Daniel T. O'Hara is a professor of English and was the first Andrew W. Mellon Term Professor in the Humanities at Temple University. He is the author of books on Yeats, visionary theory, Lionel Trilling, and radical parody. His latest book is *Empire Burlesque: The Fate of Critical Culture in Global America* (2003).